SENTIMENTAL SWEETS

Vintage Desserts from the Great Depression MADE MODERN

VALERIE SIMPSON

SPARK Publications
Charlotte, North Carolina

Sentimental Sweets
Vintage Desserts from the Great Depression Made Modern
Valerie Simpson

Designed, produced, and published by
SPARK Publications
SPARKpublications.com
Charlotte, North Carolina

Recipe Images-Valerie Simpson
Magazine Clippings-1932 issues of Good Housekeeping
Blitz Torte Cover-Amanda Loren

Printed in the United States of America

Paperback, November 2024, ISBN: 978-1-953555-81-6
Hardback, November 2024, ISBN: 978-1-953555-82-3

Library of Congress Control Number: 2024918427

DEDICATION

To the original author, whomever she was. In the most difficult of times, you completed a labor of love in recording a piece of history.

Thank you for sharing your recipes with us and generations to come.

CONTENTS

CAKES

PIES

COOKIES & CANDY

ACKNOWLEDGMENTS

INTRODUCTION

The span of years from 1914 to 1945 was arguably one of the most difficult times in US history: 1914 marked the beginning of World War I; 1945 marked the end of World War II. The Great Depression was sandwiched in the middle of this dark time.

The few remaining survivors of the Great Depression would be in their nineties today. Many of us have heard stories of this period from our grandparents and great-grandparents. Ask anyone born after 1970 what the Great Depression was, and they may answer, "Oh it was when the stock market crashed back in my grandparents' day." But it was much more than just a turn in the economy: It was a period when people of all socioeconomic levels had to call on their deepest levels of resilience. Jobs were scarce, money was scarce, and food was scarce. A popular saying was "Use it up, wear it out, make it do, or do without." The unemployment rate rose to over 24 percent. Men stood in bread lines to get food for their families, while women made clothes out of flour sacks.

There are countless stories of Americans who lost everything they had. My maternal grandfather lost all his savings due to runs on the banks. Children went hungry and barefoot. Many dropped out of school to earn money to help feed their families. To add to the hunger issue, the southern portion of the Great Plains of America was decimated by land management struggles and drought conditions that led to the Dust Bowl, resulting in devastating losses of farms, crops, and livestock.

Yet the world did not completely stop. Technological advances during this time included the differential analyzer (an early computer), the scanning electron microscope, the first jet engine, FM radio, and even sliced bread. In 1932—the year this cookbook was dated—Amelia Earhart became the first woman to fly solo nonstop coast to coast across the continental US in her Lockheed Vega. The New York Yankees defeated the Chicago Cubs in the World Series, *Grand Hotel* won the Academy Award for Best Picture, and Duke Ellington reminded us, "It Don't Mean a Thing (If It Ain't Got That Swing)."

Americans and the world recovered from the Great Depression and went on to endure more wars, more economic upturns and downturns, and an explosion in technology. Fast-forward to 2005, and one of these technologies—eBay—

Rural Alabama kitchen.

would have an unexpected but significant impact on me.

I have been an avid baker most of my life, and for what specific reason I still don't remember, I found myself looking for old cookbooks on eBay. At that time, it was not unusual for a listing to be without a picture, and I ran across an auction for a handwritten cookbook from 1932. After a nail-biting bidding war, I won it for $75. I have no idea what I expected, but what I received was an old, five-year journal with the date "May 13, 1932" written on the inside, containing about sixty dessert recipes. I use the term "recipe" loosely, as most of the recipes were just lists of ingredients. No directions. No baking times. No baking temperatures (other than the occasional directive to "bake in a slow oven"). But back in those days, most cooks assumed that one would already know how to bake a cake or a pie. Recipes were just a list of what was in it.

I have no idea who wrote the handwritten collection of recipes I have restored and am sharing with you. If this person was born in 1900 and compiled the recipes in 1932 (based on the date written inside the book) she would have already experienced World War I (1914–1918), the Roaring Twenties, Prohibition (1920–1933), the stock market crash (October 1929), and a good portion of the Great Depression (1929–1939). And most likely she would later live through World War II (1939–1945).

I fully expected that an authentic cookbook written during this period in US history would have consisted of recipes that were less than palatable. To my surprise, these recipes were anything but that. Nuts, chocolate, generous amounts of eggs and butter; these are not the ingredients of doing without. Who was this mystery woman who took the time to write down these recipes?

Judging from the smudges on most of these pages, this book was a much-used

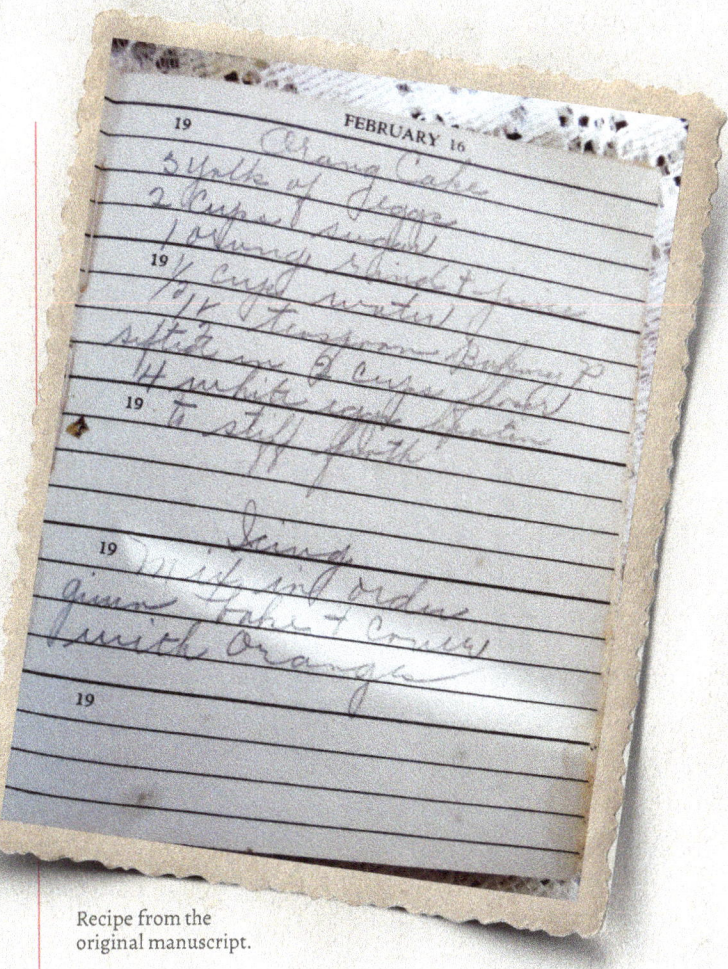

Recipe from the original manuscript.

reference. Was she an affluent person, not overly affected by the economic times? That was my first theory until I realized she had recycled an old journal to record her recipes. Victorian bakers often kept a "baker's book," which was similar to a portfolio of their recipes. Did she record her recipes in a similar manner, hoping to gain employment as a baker in someone's home or shop? Or perhaps she had known better times and was preserving these recipes for when those times returned.

It is unlikely that anyone will ever uncover the real origins of this cookbook. My aim is to draw a picture of who I have envisioned the author to be after many years of researching the era and trying to restore her original work—a work that I believe was intended to be one of hope: hope for her family, her country, and her future.

EVENTS LEADING TO THE GREAT DEPRESSION

Ask most people what caused the Great Depression, and typically their first response is to say, "The stock market crashed." On October 28, 1929, the stock market fell 13 percent; the next day it fell another 12 percent. While this was probably the single most memorable event leading to the Great Depression, this economic downfall was actually the result of a domino effect, with the dominos being set up during the 1920s.

After World War 1, the United States entered a decade of great prosperity. Manufacturing was booming, and installment payments became the norm, making it possible for consumers to afford all these products. People were buying, so manufacturers kept producing to meet the demand.

By 1929, Americans were not only buying toasters on credit, but they were also buying stock on credit. Called buying stock "on margin," stockbrokers were essentially loaning investors up to 90 percent of the stock market price. In other words, a

New York City's Wall Street around 1910.

Everett Collection / Shutterstock.com

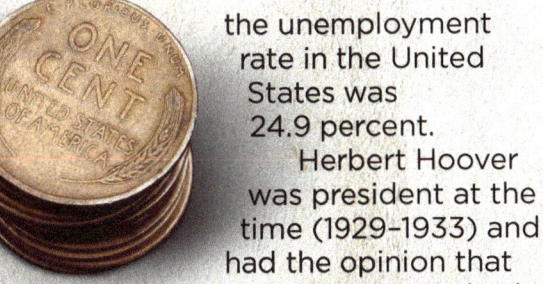

$10 investment would yield $100 worth of stock. The investors would pay back their loans with the profits from their stocks.

But in October 1929, a wobble in stock market prices caused many investors to realize that now was the time to sell, and suddenly there were more sellers of stock than there were buyers. This resulted in a panic to sell stocks while there was still some value.

The rush to sell stocks started causing the dominos to fall. Many banks had financed the broker loans that helped sell so many stocks in the first place. Investors were now pulling money from banks to cover their stock market losses. Hearing rumors that the banks were in trouble, depositors rushed to withdraw their own funds.

In 1929, as it still is today, banks used their depositors' funds to make other investments. The rapid, unplanned demand in the fall of 1929 to withdraw that deposited money had many banks coming up short in their available cash, resulting in the failure of many financial institutions. Because deposits were not insured at this time (the Federal Deposit Insurance Corporation was created by the Banking Act of 1933), many Americans lost all their savings with no chance of recovering that money.

With significantly less money on hand, Americans could no longer afford many of the items that were overproduced in the earlier, more prosperous years of the 1920s. As a result, manufacturing decreased, and workers were laid off. Many other businesses failed as well, and by 1933 the unemployment rate in the United States was 24.9 percent.

Herbert Hoover was president at the time (1929–1933) and had the opinion that things were not as bad as they seemed. He felt that individual states and local organizations—not the federal government—were responsible for caring for the people and was reluctant to provide government-funded aid. As a result, many Americans blamed Hoover for the Great Depression.

In 1932, Franklin Delano Roosevelt was elected president; in his first term, he established the New Deal, which created many federal programs to provide employment and other relief. Some of Roosevelt's programs did help the United States recover from the Great Depression.

Some economists and historians feel the Great Depression was actually over in 1933 (based on the upturn in the economy by the second quarter of that year). But it would take a decade (and arguably World War II) for the United States and the world in general to fully recover.

WHAT DID IT COST IN 1932?

My father would be shocked to go to the grocery store today (in 2024) and pay $3 for a dozen eggs, $4.32 for a pound of butter, and at least $3 for a quart of milk (prices according to Instacart)—especially considering he got milk and eggs from his own farm for a good portion of his life.

What did things cost back in the good old days? Let's look at the cost breakdown of common grocery store items in 1932, followed by a comparison of other household statistics. Changes in government policies and taxes have also impacted prices over the years: In 1932, there was no minimum wage as there is now, and gas started being taxed for the first time (1 cent per gallon) with the Revenue Act of 1932. To give some perspective, $1 in 1932 would be worth approximately $21 in 2024 (Amortization.org).

Unless otherwise noted, information was gathered from store advertisements appearing in the *Mooresville (IN) Times*, 1932–1933.

My vintage toaster.

Common Grocery Prices: 1932

Loaf of bread . . . . 5 cents
Loaf of bread, sliced . . . . 8 cents
Flour, 24-pound sack . . . . 63 cents
Sugar, 10-pound sack . . . . 47 cents
Brown sugar, 1 pound . . . . 5 cents
Vanilla extract (imitation), two 3-ounce bottles . . . . . 15 cents
Salt, 1 pound granulated. . . . . 73 cents
Baking powder, 1 pound . . . . 5 cents
Baking chocolate, ½ pound . . . . 23 cents*
Baking cocoa, ½ pound . . . . 12 cents*
Milk, 1 quart bottle . . . . 25 cents
Eggs, 1 dozen . . . . 15 cents
Cream cheese, 1 pound. . . . . 15 cents
Butter, 1 pound . . . . 24 cents
Oleo (margarine), 1 pound . . . . 10 cents
Cooking apples, 5 pounds . . . . 19 cents
Bananas, 1 pound . . . . 15 cents
Potatoes, 15 pounds . . . . 15 cents
Canned pumpkin, "2 big cans" . . . . 15 cents
Strawberry preserves, 16-ounce jar . . . . 15 cents
Jell-O, 3 packages . . . . 20 cents

Everyday Life: Then and Now

Average income $1,244 per year — $59,428 in 2023
according to Forbes.com

New house $6,500 — $387,600 in 2023
according to the National Association of Realtors

Gasoline 18 cents per gallon — $3.63 average per gallon
in 2023 according to EIA.gov

Movie ticket 35 cents — $10.78 in 2023
according to the-numbers.com

Postage 3 cents — 66 cents according to USPS.com

New car $622 — $48,451 in 2023
according to Kelley Blue Book

US population 124,840,472 — 2023 population 334,914,895
according to census.gov

Life expectancy 62.3 years — 76.4 years
for both sexes in 2023 according to cdc.gov

Evening Star (Washington, DC), February 13, 1933.

CHOPPING WOOD OR SHOVELING COAL:

Rural vs. Urban Baking

As I've considered what life was like for the original author of these recipes, my initial theory was that she likely lived in an urban area because many of the ingredients she used probably would have been difficult to acquire without a well-stocked general store.

She could very well have had electric appliances. William Hadaway received the first patent for an electric stove in 1896, and by the 1920s the electric stove was competing with the gas stove for home use. Coal-burning stoves were also in use at this time, but these required coal delivery and storage and would have made maintaining the desired cooking temperatures difficult.

She may have still used an icebox for food preservation, but it is possible that she could have had an electric refrigerator, as refrigerators became more common in private homes by the late 1920s. Electric toasters and vacuum cleaners were also available. Running water and indoor plumbing were commonly available in urban areas by the 1930s. The Sunbeam Mixmaster was introduced in 1930, so perhaps the urban baker was no longer whipping egg whites and heavy cream by hand! (We always had a Mixmaster when I was growing up.)

More affluent homes may have had servants to help with cooking and housekeeping, but the economic downturn of the period forced many households to dismiss their servants simply because they could no longer afford them.

Rural baking was much more challenging. It was not until 1936 that Congress passed the Rural Electrification Act, which helped provide the funding for farmers to bring electricity to their rural areas. No electricity meant no electric toasters, Mixmasters, or stoves.

Chances are she was still baking on a wood-burning stove and bringing water inside from an outdoor well. As with a coal stove, a woodburning stove required great effort to maintain a consistent temperature. The physical effort involved in fueling a woodburning stove was no easy task either; someone had to cut down the tree, chop and stack the wood, and haul it inside.

A 1930s rural baker procured many needed ingredients herself: milk from her cows, butter that she churned by hand, eggs from her own hens, and fruit and nuts from her own trees. Flour and sugar were purchased from a general store, which may have required a considerable effort to get to.

Baking in the 1930s was an involved necessity, but it was clearly a labor of love for the original author whether she lived on a farm or in the city.

KITCHENETTES, PROHIBITION, AND BATHTUB GIN

The form and function of urban American kitchens was changing by 1932, with fewer cakes being made there. Jane Ziegelman and Andrew Coe discuss this altered kitchen setting in their book *A Square Meal: A Culinary History of The Great Depression*. To properly set the stage, we must go back a few years earlier to post–World War I and the Roaring Twenties.

World War I provided many opportunities for women to work outside the home, either to fill vacancies left by men enlisting in the armed forces or to fill new positions created by the war effort. After World War I ended, many women continued to work outside the home.

In bigger cities, such as Chicago and New York, efficiency apartments were popular. These apartments had every inch of their square footage optimized for efficiency. The reduced size of the living area meant women could manage their housekeeping without the need of servants. The small, compact cooking area of these homes was referred to as a kitchenette. However, the compact size of these kitchens made cooking more difficult, as there was very little space for working. Storing all the modern electric appliances homemakers now owned was also a challenge.

With many women working all day outside the home, they were not eager to come home and cook. The solution: meals planned around canned goods. *The Busy Woman's Cookbook* (1925) offered many meal plans incorporating canned goods. This was also the time that the corner deli became popular, altogether alleviating the need for cooking.

Some urbanites were even able to find an alternate use for their kitchenettes. Prohibition was still in effect in 1932, and many kitchenettes were turned into mini bars, serving bootleg liquor (or maybe some homemade bathtub gin) instead of dinner!

Food for thought:
Vanilla extract can be up to 35 percent alcohol. So was vanilla extract available during this time period? The answer is yes. Vanilla extract is considered non-potable, meaning you can't (or shouldn't) drink it, so it was exempt from the alcohol ban during the Prohibition years (1920–1933).

VINTAGE MEASUREMENTS

While attempting to restore the recipes in the journal, I ran across some interesting measurements: butter the size of an egg, 3 sifts of flour, 10 cents worth of nuts, a waterglass full of honey.

Fannie Farmer invented the dry measuring cup in 1896. Cooks before that and for many years going forward tended to implement whatever kitchen tools they had to serve as a basis for measuring. How many times have we heard someone say, "My Grandmother never measured anything."

If cooks did measure anything, their "equipment" might include a teacup, wineglass, and almost any type of spoon, including a coffee spoon, dessert spoon, or cooking spoon. The baker's hand was the most convenient measuring unit and could be used as a fistful, a handful, or just a pinch.

As of this writing my own mother is ninety-two years old. Growing up, I don't remember us ever owning a set of measuring spoons; my mother most likely learned her measuring methods from my grandmother. The soup spoon was the tablespoon, and the kitchen spoon was the teaspoon. We did have a standardized measuring cup, and we always sifted our dry ingredients—another step probably learned from my grandmother. In those days, my grandmother would have had to purchase larger, less refined bags of flour, so sifting was important to break up the clumps. (**Baking hint:** Sifting your dry ingredients prior to mixing incorporates air into your mixture, giving your cake greater "lift".)

Below are some common vintage measurements and their modern approximate equivalents:

- Sift of flour ≈ 1 cup of flour
- Butter the size of an egg ≈ ¼ cup
- Water glass ≈ 8 ounces
- Teacup ≈ ½ to ¾ cup
- Wineglass ≈ ¼ cup
- Handful ≈ ½ cup
- Fistful ≈ ¼ cup
- Cooking spoon ≈ 3 teaspoons
- Dessert spoon ≈ 2 teaspoons
- Kitchen spoon ≈ 1 teaspoon
- Coffee spoon ≈ ½ teaspoon
- Pinch ≈ $\frac{1}{16}$ to ⅛ teaspoon

Vintage Oven Temperatures

Bakers of this era also faced challenges with oven temperatures. I realized immediately that very few recipes in the original journal included directions with cooking temperatures. There was the occasional reference to "bake in a slow oven." I was quite surprised at this omission, but I had not considered that bakers could be using a wood-burning stove, a coal-burning stove, a gas stove, or an electric stove, each with its unique set of challenges in maintaining baking temperatures.

Vintage Oven Settings

Description	Temperature
Cool oven	200°F
Very slow oven	250°F
Slow oven	300–325°F
Moderately slow	325–350°F
Moderate oven	350–375°F
Moderately hot	375–400°F
Hot oven	400–450°F
Very hot or fast oven	450–500°F

As you can see from the table above, oven settings can vary from 25 to 50 degrees. Modern bakers can still run into similar issues, as today's more advanced ovens can have the same variations in oven settings: 350 degrees set on your oven may in reality be 325 degrees or 375 degrees. This is discussed more in the section on "Tips for Better Baking."

BUTTER, LARD, AND OLEO

A baker in 1932 had at least three choices for the source of fat they could use in their recipes: butter, lard, and oleo margarine.

Butter cost approximately 24 cents per pound in 1932. If you had a cow, it was essentially free, but first you had to milk the cow and then churn the butter. My father, who was fourteen years old in 1932, would always tell childhood stories of how he would milk the cow by hand and then, as soon as the bucket was full, the cow would kick it over.

But milking the cow wasn't the only time-consuming part of the process: Churning butter could take anywhere from fifteen to forty-five minutes using a hand churn. This did not include the time to process the butter, which still required several more steps.

Lard was another option and more economical at 15 cents for two pounds. Urban bakers purchased it from their local grocer or butcher, of course, whereas rural bakers most likely rendered their own.

Modern bakers often turn up their noses at lard, fearing it an unhealthy choice. But surprisingly, lard contains more monounsaturated fat and oleic acid than butter and less saturated fat than butter. Lard also tends to produce a flakier pie crust than butter. There were some cookie recipes in this book that called for lard, so in keeping with the spirit of the times I did make some test batches with lard. They turned out surprisingly moist.

Oleo margarine was also available. Invented in 1869 by a French chemist, it consisted of tallow and lard. Since it was cheaper than butter, it was often used instead of butter during the Great Depression and during World War II when butter was in short supply. Today's margarine (my mother still calls it oleo) is plant based and can be substituted for butter, but typically the baking results are not as good, especially if tub margarine is used instead of the sticks.

When using butter, most bakers today just choose between salted and unsalted. The salt in butter acts as a preservative so that it will have a longer shelf life, but many bakers prefer unsalted butter in order to have more control over the flavor of the baked good. If you decide to go with salted butter, you can usually omit any additional salt called for in the recipe.

Photograph by author of personal butter churn.

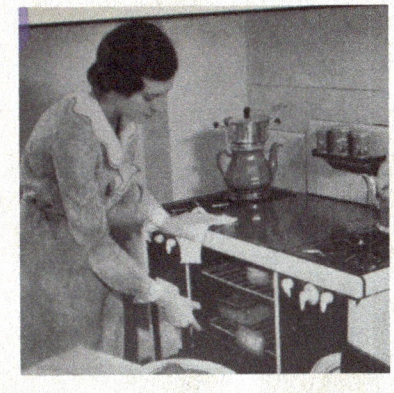

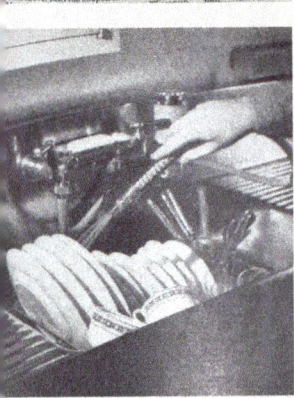

IS IT CAKE YET?

Baking Times and How to Tell If It's Done

I cannot overemphasize how important it is to know how to test a cake for doneness. Ovens will vary in exact temperatures (in my own oven, the light indicates it's preheated, but it's really only 200 degrees). You probably have areas in your oven that are hotter than others. And the size of the pan, the depth of the pan, and even the material of the pan can all affect your baking times.

Before you even start to bake a cake, you need to know if your oven temperature is really what it says on the dial. Invest in an oven thermometer. It is an inexpensive tool, and it will save you from many a failed cake. If your oven is set at 350 degrees but the oven thermometer won't go above 325, then you are not going to be able to rely on the baking times specified in a recipe and will have to add or subtract time depending on the actual temperature reading.

How do you test for doneness?

I rely on three factors to tell if my cake is done:

1. The cake should gently spring back if you lightly touch the top of your cake before you take it out of the oven. If there's batter on your fingers, it's not ready yet.
2. The edges should be slightly pulling away from the sides of the pan.

Here's a quick reference chart of baking times and temperatures for common pans. (Note that these are useful as a general rule of thumb, as recipes will vary.)

Pan Type	Oven Temperature	Cooking Time
Cupcake	350°F	18–25 minutes
Layer Cake	350°F	25–35 minutes
Springform Pan (9")	350°F	25–35 minutes
Loaf Cake	350°F	45–55 minutes
Angel Food Cake	350°F	45–55 minutes
Bundt Cake	350°F	45–55 minutes

3. A cake tester inserted in the middle of the cake should come out clean, meaning there is no batter on the cake tester when you pull it out.

Another way to test is to check the cake with a food thermometer. It should read about 210 degrees when the cake is done.

I start checking for doneness about 5 minutes before the timer goes off, and I continue to add time incrementally until I am certain my cake is done. A word of caution: Don't start checking too soon. The sudden change in temperature can cause your cake to fall. Turn on your oven light and check through the window to make sure your cake has definitely risen and looks set *before* you open the door.

The material your baking pans are made of can also affect baking time. Glass pans tend to take longer to heat than metal, and that can cause the sides of your cake to bake too fast. They also cool down more slowly, meaning your cake could continue to bake a few minutes after you take the cake out. Metal pans cool faster than glass pans, so typically your cake will stop baking very shortly after removing it from the oven. Darker metal pans tend to absorb more heat than lighter metal pans.

What about silicone pans?

I have had variable results with silicone cake pans, especially silicone Bundt-style pans. Silicone doesn't conduct heat the way that metal does, which can cause your cake to bake unevenly. (Truth be told, the last time I used a silicone cake pan was . . . the *last* time I used a silicone cake pan. Save silicone pans for Jell-O molds!)

To sum it up, baking times stated in a recipe are approximate. You can use the best ingredients and measure with scientific precision, but if your cake is not done or if it's overbaked, you won't enjoy eating it.

TIPS FOR BETTER BAKING

There are literally hundreds of books out there that can teach you how to bake; this is not one of them. However, there are some tips I can share with you to help ensure your attempts are successful.

Read the recipe. First and foremost, read the entire recipe *before* you even set out your baking equipment. Make sure you understand what you need to do in each step. Have the correct ingredients and proper equipment, and allow enough time to prepare your ingredients as well. For example, my Poppy Seed Pie recipe calls for you to soak the poppy seeds overnight—that can't happen if you are trying to throw a pie together at the last minute.

Know your oven. Preheat your oven to the temperature stated in the recipe, and then wait another 5 to 10 minutes before putting your uncooked recipe in. Are you sure that when you set it at 350 degrees, it's not actually 325 degrees or 375 degrees? You can have your oven professionally calibrated, but that can get pricey. Instead, invest in an inexpensive oven thermometer that you can hang from one of the racks. You might be surprised what you find—for example, if you've wondered why it always takes your cakes longer to bake than the recipe says, now you'll know.

Test for doneness. Due to multiple variables—including factors such as the weather, the temperature of the ingredients, the age of the cake pan, and the location of the pan in the oven—your baking times may vary, even if you have baked that same cake a hundred times before. Baking times are a guide; test for doneness to know for certain when a cake is

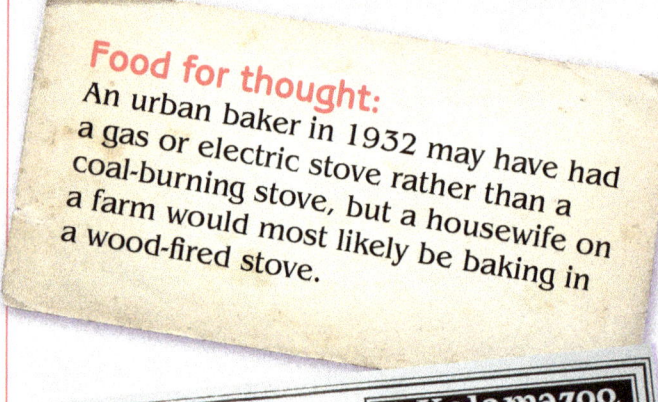

Food for thought:
An urban baker in 1932 may have had a gas or electric stove rather than a coal-burning stove, but a housewife on a farm would most likely be baking in a wood-fired stove.

ready. A cake tester or knife inserted in the middle of a cake should come out clean as you remove it. Your cake should be just pulling away from the sides of the pan. It should also spring back when touched. Still not sure? You can invest in a cake thermometer for less than $15.

Have the right equipment. A baker in even the most well-equipped kitchen in 1932 would certainly marvel at the endless assortment of baking equipment available today. Now this does not mean you need to own every baking pan and kitchen gadget ever produced (although I have made great strides toward accomplishing this).

Buying the right equipment does not need to be expensive either. For example, you can purchase a handheld mixer for $25 or so, and used or refurbished stand mixers are easy to find online for a fair price. A decent mixer will make a significant difference in your baking experience—there is no way you are going to want to whip egg whites by hand. Likewise, you can often find quality used baking pans online or at thrift stores. I like the heavier nonstick pans. A Bundt-style pan, a pie pan (not glass!), and a couple of layer pans are all you need to start. And while you could purchase a timer, you could also just use the timer on your phone at no extra cost.

Properly prepare your cake pans prior to baking. Nothing is more frustrating than having a beautiful cake stick to the pan. This is where parchment paper is your best friend. Cut a circle the size of the bottom of your cake pan. Put a dab of cooking spray or butter on the parchment circle to adhere it to the bottom of the pan (I have had the parchment slip as I was pouring batter into the pan).

Here is a list of basic baking equipment to get you started:

- Stand or handheld mixer
- Quality baking pans
- Easy-to-read measuring cup
- Set of measuring spoons
- Nonstick cooking spray
- Parchment paper
- Scissors
- Cooling rack
- Baking mitts
- Large spatula
- Large rolling pin
- Timer

Spray the sides generously with cooking oil spray, or you can go old school and grease the sides of the pan with butter or shortening. I love my Bundt pans, but the nooks and crannies of the intricately designed ones can be a problem. Be aware of these areas and make sure you don't miss any when greasing your pan. Mix your ingredients well, but don't overmix. Stop your mixer about a minute after you have added all ingredients, and scrape down the sides with a spatula to make sure all of your ingredients are well incorporated. And there's nothing wrong finishing by hand mixing to make sure you don't overmix.

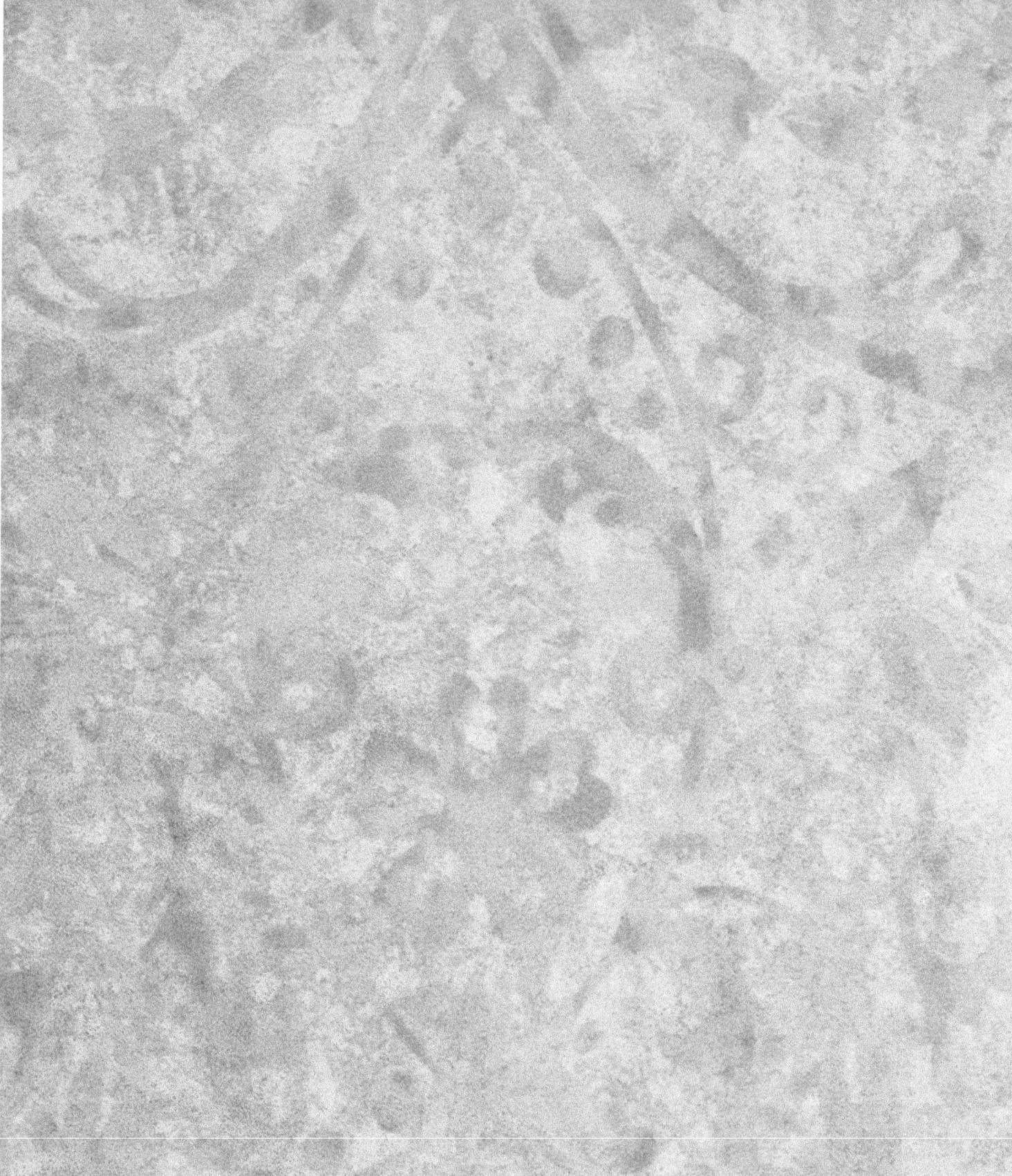

CAKE

WHY SO MANY BUNDT PANS?

Bundt pans are very heavily utilized in these recipes! I wanted to showcase the original cake recipes as much as possible, and many of the recipes didn't include any icings or toppings. I purposely kept the decorations simple for the same reason. Most of the Bundt recipes could easily be converted into layer cakes with your favorite icings or fillings. The original journal had many of the icings listed separately, so I have a feeling the author mixed and matched cakes and icings to suit the occasion. For cake decorators, your favorite buttercream icing could be substituted in most of the cake recipes.

WHERE DID THE BUNDT CAKE ORIGINATE?

The actual Bundt pan did not come into production until 1950. Prior to that, a baker probably would have used a tube pan to get a large, non-layered cake.

Before there was either the tube pan or the Bundt pan, there was the Gugelhupf or Kugelhopf cake. Possibly originating in Austria in the late 1700s, it is said to have been a favorite of Marie Antoinette. This cake resembles a modern-day Bundt cake but is leavened with yeast instead of egg whites, baking powder or baking soda. The sides of the pan have distinctive fluting like a Bundt pan, but a Kugelhopf pan tends to be taller than a Bundt pan. The taller sides will give the yeast dough more room to rise.

Bakers in the 1930s would have been using a tube pan or angel food pan for sponge-type cakes. Cakes that use egg whites for leavening, such as angel food cakes, need the straight sides to "grab" as the cake rises. This is the reason you **do not** grease a tube pan when making an angel food cake, as the grease will prevent the egg whites from "sticking" to the sides and your cake won't rise. The tube in the middle adds more surface area for the batter to stick to, also helping your angel food cake rise.

The actual Bundt pan was invented in 1950 by H. David Dalquist, who owned Nordic Ware.

He cast the pan for a group of women who were trying to recreate the Kugelhopf cake. But it wasn't until 1966 that the Bundt pan was in high demand. That was the year a Bundt cake—the Tunnel of Fudge Cake—placed second in the seventeenth annual Pillsbury Bake Off.

I chose Bundt pans for many of the recipes as they don't require much to decorate. Almost any two-layer cake recipe will do well in a Bundt pan. The hole in the middle helps conduct heat, allowing the cake to bake more evenly. Just be sure to adjust your baking times. The deeper pan will take longer to bake than layer cakes, usually requiring at least 45 to 50 minutes. Once out of the oven, a dusting of powdered sugar, a drizzle of thin icing glaze, or even a basting of warmed fruit preserves is all you'll need to finish it.

Food for thought:
The first detailed recipe of an angel food cake was published in the Boston Cooking School Cook Book in 1884.

TORTE OR CAKE?

What is the difference between a torte and a cake?

Many of the orginal recipes contained the word "torte" in the title. Most people think of a torte as a multilayer cake with some sort of filling between the layers. But the ingredients also distinguish a torte from a cake: Torte ingredients are typically denser than those used in a cake, and often there is very little to no flour used in a true torte recipe. The Cheese Torte recipe in this book, for example, calls for only ¼ cup flour, and the texture is denser than that of a traditional cheesecake.

In keeping with the spirit of the original author, I left most of the titles as they were in the journal. I have no idea if she knew the difference or why some recipes that are clearly cakes were called tortes. That same Cheese Torte recipe that uses only a small amount of flour actually does not even have layers as we would expect for a dessert called a torte.

Nevertheless, by any name, they all taste delicious!

The phrase **"torte a cake"** means to slice a cake horizontally into many layers.

GRAHAM CRACKERS AND THE TEMPERANCE MOVEMENT

Graham crackers are made from graham flour, which is a coarse-ground whole wheat flour. It was named after Sylvester Graham (1794–1851), a Presbyterian minister.

In the 1830s, a social movement called the temperance movement was in full swing, promoting total abstinence from alcoholic beverages. (It was this temperance movement in the United States that led to Prohibition.)

Sylvester Graham took the temperance movement one step further and encouraged his followers to abstain from anything that might elicit physical pleasure, including delicious foods. He even went so far as to develop his own (bland) dietary guidelines that placed an emphasis on vegetarianism. He decided this diet needed some supplementation, so he created the graham cracker (made from graham flour, of course) and designed it to be as bland as possible.

The original cookbook included three cake recipes that called for graham crackers. These recipes are anything but bland or boring, and I am happy to say that I don't think Sylvester Graham would have approved!

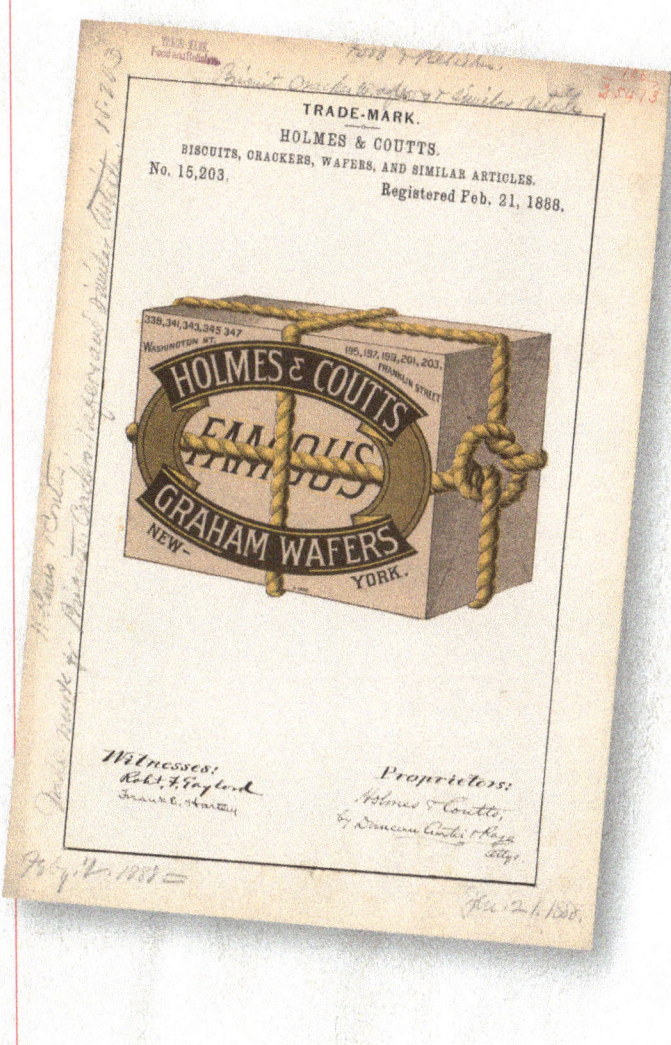

Graham Cracker Torte

*This turned out to be surprisingly good! I added a coconut custard filling
to the original recipe and topped the torte with an almond glaze.*

Ingredients

Cake:

1 cup cake flour, sifted

1 teaspoon baking powder

1 cup finely crushed
graham cracker crumbs

1 cup (2 sticks) unsalted
butter, room temperature

1 cup granulated sugar

½ cup light or dark brown
sugar, lightly packed

2 large eggs, well beaten,
room temperature

1 teaspoon almond extract

1 cup whole milk,
room temperature

Coconut Custard Filling:

1 cup whole milk,
room temperature

2 large egg yolks, well
beaten, room temperature

½ cup granulated sugar

¼ cup flaked coconut
(optional)

1 to 2 tablespoons
tablespoon cornstarch

1 teaspoon almond extract

Almond Glaze:

3 cups powdered sugar, sifted

1 cup whole milk or heavy
cream, room temperature

1 teaspoon almond extract

¼ cup sliced almonds
(optional garnish)

Directions

1. Preheat the oven to 350 degrees. Grease the sides of two 8- or 9-inch layer pans and line the bottoms with parchment paper. Sift together the cake flour and baking powder. Add the graham cracker crumbs and stir well to combine; set aside.

2. Using an electric mixer with a paddle attachment, cream the butter, granulated sugar, and brown sugar on medium speed, 2 to 3 minutes. Add the eggs and almond extract. Alternate adding the flour mixture and the milk, then stop the mixer and scrape down the sides of the bowl with a spatula to make sure all ingredients are thoroughly combined. Finish mixing by hand to avoid overmixing.

3. Divide the batter evenly between the two cake pans. Bake for 25 to 35 minutes, until a cake tester inserted in the middle comes out clean. Transfer to a wire cooling rack; cool in the pans for 10 to 15 minutes before turning out the layers onto the rack to cool completely.

4. To prepare the coconut custard filling, combine the milk, egg yolks, sugar, and optional flaked coconut in a saucepan over medium heat; sift in the cornstarch with a cake sifter or tea strainer to prevent clumping. Do not allow the mixture to boil. Stir constantly, scraping the bottom of the pan so that nothing sticks. Add additional cornstarch if a thicker consistency is desired, but the mixture will thicken as it cools. Remove from the heat when it is almost a pudding-like consistency; stir in the almond extract. Cool completely.

5. To make the almond glaze, use an electric mixer on low speed to combine the powdered sugar, cream, and almond extract. Gradually increase the mixer speed until ingredients are thoroughly blended to a smooth consistancy then stop the mixer and scrape down the sides of the bowl as needed to make sure all ingredients are well combined. Adjust the consistency of the glaze by adding more powdered sugar to thicken or more cream to thin it out.

6. To assemble the cake once the cake layers and custard have cooled, spread the custard filling on top of one cake layer; cover with the second cake layer. Drizzle the almond glaze over the cake. Garnish with sliced almonds, if desired.

Graham Cracker Cake

Light and moist, with the perfect taste of
graham crackers. Serve as is, or top with a chocolate glaze.

Ingredients

Cake:

1 cup cake flour, sifted

2 teaspoons baking powder

½ teaspoon salt

1 cup finely crushed graham cracker crumbs

1 cup chopped walnuts

½ cup (1 stick) unsalted butter, room temperature

1 cup granulated sugar

2 large eggs, separated, room temperature

1 teaspoon vanilla extract

1 cup whole milk, room temperature

Chocolate Glaze Icing:

1½ cups powdered sugar, sifted

¼ cup unsweetened cocoa powder, sifted

2 tablespoons whole milk or heavy cream, room temperature

1 teaspoon vanilla extract

Walnut halves (optional garnish)

Directions

1. Preheat the oven to 350 degrees. Liberally grease a 10-inch (10- to 12-cup) Bundt pan and dust with flour; tap the inverted pan to remove excess flour. Sift together the cake flour, baking powder, and salt; mix in the graham cracker crumbs and walnuts. Set aside.

2. Using an electric mixer with a paddle attachment, cream the butter and sugar on medium speed until light and creamy, 2 to 3 minutes. Beat the two egg yolks and add to the mixture; add the vanilla extract. Alternate adding the sifted flour mixture and the milk. Stop the mixer and scrape down the sides of the bowl with a spatula to make sure all ingredients are well incorporated. Finish mixing by hand to avoid overmixing.

3. In a separate bowl, use an electric mixer on high speed to beat the 2 egg whites until stiff peaks form, 4 to 5 minutes. With a spatula, gently fold the beaten egg whites into the batter until just mixed, taking care not to overmix and "knock" the air out of the egg whites, which would prevent the cake from fully rising.

4. Pour the batter into the prepared pan; bake for 45 to 55 minutes, until a cake tester inserted in the middle comes out clean. Transfer to a wire cooling rack; cool in the pan for 10 to 15 minutes before inverting the cake onto the rack. Remove the pan and allow the cake to cool completely, then serve plain or add a chocolate glaze icing.

5. To make the chocolate glaze icing, sift together the powdered sugar and cocoa powder in a medium bowl. Slowly stir in the milk and vanilla extract a little at a time to make a smooth, pourable glaze. Drizzle over the cooled cake. Garnish with walnut halves, if desired.

Potato Cake

Don't let the title fool you! This is one of the best chocolate cakes you'll ever have. The addition of the mashed potato makes this an incredibly moist cake. Serve as is, or top with a chocolate glaze.

Ingredients

Cake:

1 small russet potato
(½ cup mashed)

1 cup cake flour, sifted

3 tablespoons unsweetened cocoa powder, sifted

1 teaspoon baking powder

1 teaspoon baking soda

Pinch of salt

½ cup (1 stick) unsalted butter, room temperature

1 cup granulated sugar

2 large eggs, well beaten, room temperature

½ cup whole milk, room temperature

1 teaspoon vanilla extract

1 cup finely chopped walnuts

Chocolate Glaze:

1½ cups powdered sugar, sifted

¼ cup unsweetened cocoa powder, sifted

2 tablespoons whole milk or water, room temperature

1 teaspoon vanilla extract

Plan ahead

1. Peel and cook 1 small russet potato, enough to make ½ cup mashed potato. Allow to cool before using in the recipe.

Directions

2. Preheat the oven to 350 degrees. Liberally grease a 10-inch (10- to 12-cup) Bundt pan and dust with flour; tap the inverted pan to remove excess flour. Sift together the cake flour, cocoa powder, baking powder, baking soda, and salt.

3. Using an electric mixer with a paddle attachment, cream the butter and sugar on medium speed until light and fluffy, 2 to 3 minutes; add the beaten eggs, then the cooled mashed potato. Alternate adding the sifted flour mixture and the milk. Stop the mixer and scrape down the sides of the bowl with a spatula to make sure all ingredients are well mixed. Add the vanilla extract and chopped walnuts. Finish mixing by hand to avoid overmixing.

4. Pour the batter into the prepared pan; bake for 45 to 55 minutes, until a cake tester inserted in the middle comes out clean. Transfer to a wire cooling rack; cool in the pan for 10 to 15 minutes before inverting the cake onto the rack. Remove the pan and allow the cake to cool completely before icing.

5. To make the chocolate glaze, sift together the powdered sugar and cocoa powder in a medium bowl. Slowly stir in the milk and vanilla extract a little at a time to make a smooth, pourable glaze. Pour over the cooled cake.

Slate Cake

I have no idea where this cake got its name, but if you like oatmeal cookies, you'll love this cake version that's great as a breakfast treat or an afternoon tea cake. Serve plain or with cinnamon cream cheese icing.

Ingredients

Cake:

2 cups cake flour, sifted

1 teaspoon baking powder

1 teaspoon baking soda

1 teaspoon ground cinnamon

½ teaspoon salt

1 cup (2 sticks) unsalted butter, room temperature

2 cups light or dark brown sugar, lightly packed

1½ cups sour milk (see note) or buttermilk, room temperature

1 teaspoon vanilla extract

2 cups old-fashioned rolled oats

½ cup chopped pecans or walnuts

Cinnamon Cream Cheese Icing:

8 ounces full-fat cream cheese, room temperature

½ cup (1 stick) unsalted butter, room temperature

2 cups powdered sugar, sifted

¼ cup whole milk or heavy cream, room temperature

1 teaspoon vanilla extract

1 teaspoon ground cinnamon

Chopped pecans or walnuts for garnish

Directions

1. Preheat the oven to 350 degrees. Liberally grease a 10-inch (10- to 12-cup) Bundt pan and dust with flour; tap the inverted pan to remove excess flour. Sift together the cake flour, baking powder, baking soda, cinnamon, and salt; set aside.

2. Using an electric mixer with a paddle attachment, cream the butter and brown sugar on medium speed until light and fluffy, 2 to 3 minutes. Alternate adding the sifted flour mixture and the sour milk; then add the vanilla extract, oats, and nuts. Stop the mixer and scrape down the sides of the bowl with a spatula to make sure all ingredients are well incorporated. Finish mixing by hand to prevent overmixing.

3. Pour the batter into the prepared pan and bake. Check for doneness after 40 minutes; it may require an additional 5 to 15 minutes, until a cake tester inserted in the middle of the cake comes out clean. Do not overbake the cake as it will come out dry. Transfer to a wire cooling rack; cool in the pan for 10 to 15 minutes before inverting the cake onto the rack. Remove the pan and allow the cake to cool completely before icing.

4. To make the cinnamon cream cheese icing, use an electric mixer on medium speed to combine the cream cheese, powdered sugar, milk, vanilla extract, and cinnamon until smooth; add extra cinnamon, if desired. For a thinner consistency, add more milk; to thicken, add more powdered sugar. Drizzle the icing over the cooled cake; top with additional chopped pecans or walnuts.

Note: To replicate sour milk, add 1 tablespoon white vinegar or lemon juice to 1 cup whole milk; allow it to stand for at least 5 minutes before using. Buttermilk can be substituted (omit the vinegar or lemon juice) and will give a slightly richer texture. The original recipe calls for sour milk. In the days of the Great Depression, nothing was wasted, so a cake was a good way to use up old or sour milk. In the spirit of the original recipes, I mainly use replicated sour milk.

Tutti Frutti Cake

In the original manuscript there were two versions of this recipe: Both had very similar ingredients, but only one called for a custard filling. And the custard filling makes this cake downright decadent. OK, the chocolate frosting was my idea. You can omit it entirely or just drizzle some melted dark chocolate over the cake. Either way, it's yummy!

Ingredients

Cake:

1 teaspoon baking soda

1 tablespoon white vinegar

½ cup (1 stick) unsalted butter, room temperature

1 cup light or dark brown sugar, lightly packed

1 large egg, well beaten, room temperature

1 teaspoon vanilla extract

1½ cups cake flour, sifted

1 cup sour milk (see note) or buttermilk, room temperature

½ cup chopped walnuts

½ cup chopped pitted dates

Custard Filling:

2 cups whole milk, room temperature

1 teaspoon unsalted butter, room temperature

2 large egg yolks, room temperature

¼ to ½ cup granulated sugar

1 to 2 tablespoons cornstarch

1 teaspoon vanilla extract

Chocolate Cream Cheese Icing:

3½ cups powdered sugar, sifted

⅔ cup unsweetened cocoa powder, sifted

Pinch of salt

12 ounces full-fat cream cheese, room temperature

¾ cup (1½ sticks) unsalted butter, room temperature

1 teaspoon vanilla extract

1 to 2 tablespoons whole milk or heavy cream, room temperature

Directions

1. Preheat the oven to 350 degrees. Grease the sides of two 8- or 9-inch layer cake pans and line the bottoms with parchment paper. Dissolve the baking soda in the vinegar; set aside.

2. Using an electric mixer with a paddle attachment, cream the butter and brown sugar on medium speed until light and fluffy, 2 to 3 minutes. Add the beaten egg and vanilla; mix well, but do not overbeat. Add the cake flour, baking soda solution, and milk. Stop the mixer and scrape the sides of the bowl with a spatula to make sure all ingredients are well mixed. Add the walnuts and dates.

3. Divide the batter equally between the two cake pans; bake for 25 to 35 minutes, until a cake tester inserted in the middle comes out clean. Transfer to a wire cooling rack; cool in the pans for 10 to 15 minutes before turning out the layers onto the rack to cool completely.

4. To prepare the custard filling, heat the milk and butter in a saucepan over medium heat until simmering, stirring constantly. Remove the mixture from the heat before it comes to a boil.

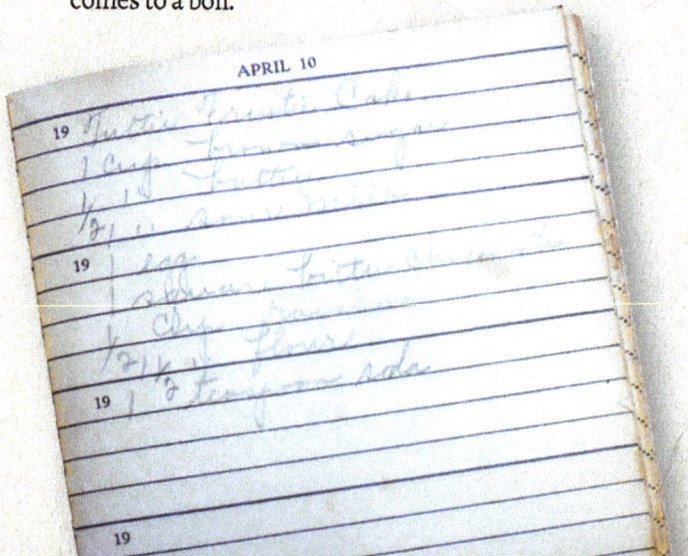

5. In a separate bowl, whisk the yolks, granulated sugar, and cornstarch until the sugar dissolves. (**Tip:** To prevent lumps from the cornstarch, sift the cornstarch into the mixture using a cake sifter or a tea strainer.)

6. Return the saucepan to a low heat. Pour in the egg mixture a little at a time to avoid curdling. Whisk continuously until the custard thickens, 8 to 10 minutes. Add the vanilla extract just as you remove the pan from the heat; if desired, add extra vanilla to suit taste. Allow the custard to cool completely.

7. To make the chocolate cream cheese icing, first sift together the powdered sugar, cocoa powder, and salt; set aside. Using an electric mixer on high speed, beat the cream cheese and butter until smooth and creamy, about 1 minute. Slowly add the sifted powdered sugar mixture, vanilla extract, and milk until thoroughly combined. Add more milk if needed to obtain the desired icing consistency.

8. To assemble once the cake and custard are completely cool, spread the custard filling on top of one cake layer; place the second cake layer over the custard. Cover with chocolate cream cheese icing.

Note: To replicate sour milk, add 1 tablespoon white vinegar or lemon juice to 1 cup whole milk; allow it to stand for at least 5 minutes before using. Buttermilk can be substituted (omit the vinegar or lemon juice) and will give a slightly richer texture. The original recipe calls for sour milk. In the days of the Great Depression, nothing was wasted, so a cake was a good way to use up old or sour milk. In the spirit of the original recipes, I mainly use replicated sour milk.

Variation: Omit the custard. Bake the cake in a 10-cup Bundt pan at 350 degrees for 45 to 55 minutes. Drizzle the cooled cake with melted dark chocolate.

Walnut Ribbon Cake

A bit of chocolate and some chopped walnuts make this a moist, rich (not too sweet) cake with a hint of orange flavoring. The plain version of this cake is delicious on its own, or try it topped with a chocolate orange glaze. Of all the recipes in the original manuscript, this one had the most smudges. I think it must have been a favorite!

Ingredients

Cake:

2¼ cups cake flour, sifted

1¼ teaspoons baking soda

1 teaspoon baking powder

1 cup (2 sticks) unsalted butter, room temperature

1 cup granulated sugar

2 large egg yolks + 2 large eggs, well beaten, room temperature

1 teaspoon vanilla extract

1 ounce (28 g) semisweet baking chocolate, melted

1 cup orange juice, room temperature

1 cup chopped walnuts

Additional walnut halves or chopped walnuts for garnish (optional)

Orange slices for garnish (optional)

Chocolate Orange Glaze:

1½ cups powdered sugar, sifted

¼ cup unsweetened cocoa powder, sifted

2 tablespoons whole milk or water, room temperature

1 to 2 teaspoons orange extract

½ teaspoon orange zest (optional)

Directions

1. Preheat the oven to 350 degrees. Liberally grease a 10-inch (10- to 12-cup) Bundt pan and dust with flour; tap the inverted pan to remove excess flour. Sift together the cake flour, baking soda, and baking powder; set aside.

2. Using an electric mixer with a paddle attachment, cream the butter and sugar on medium speed until light and fluffy, 2 to 3 minutes. Mix in the beaten yolks and eggs until just incorporated. Add the vanilla extract, then the melted chocolate. Alternate mixing in the sifted flour mixture and the orange juice; add the chopped nuts. Stop the mixer and scrape down the sides of the bowl with a spatula to make sure all ingredients are well incorporated. Finish mixing by hand to avoid overmixing.

3. Pour the batter into the prepared pan; bake for 45 to 55 minutes, until a cake tester inserted in the middle comes out clean. Transfer to a wire cooling rack; cool in the pan for 10 to 15 minutes before inverting the cake onto the rack. Remove the pan and allow the cake to cool completely.

4. To make the chocolate orange glaze, sift together the powdered sugar and cocoa powder in a medium bowl. Slowly stir in the milk, orange extract, and optional orange zest to make a smooth, pourable glaze. Adjust the amounts of orange extract and zest to suit your taste. Drizzle the glaze over the cooled cake. Garnish with additional walnuts and/or orange slices, if desired.

Farina Torte

This surprisingly moist cake—which uses soaked farina cereal instead of flour—was a big hit during a family night of recipe sampling. This is delicious with mandarin orange slices, but feel free to substitute another fresh fruit.

Ingredients

Cake:

1 cup farina cereal, soaked overnight (see note)

1 cup whole milk

4 large eggs, separated, room temperature

2 cups granulated sugar

⅔ cup chopped walnuts

1 teaspoon baking powder

2 teaspoons all-purpose flour

1 teaspoon vanilla extract

Mandarin orange segments

Whipped Cream:

1 cup heavy whipping cream, very cold

1 teaspoon vanilla extract

1 tablespoon powdered sugar, sifted

Plan ahead

1. Soak 1 cup farina cereal in 1 cup whole milk overnight in the refrigerator; allow the mixture to come to room temperature before using.

Directions

2. Preheat the oven to 350 degrees. Grease the sides of two 8- or 9-inch layer cake pans and line the bottoms with parchment paper. Chill a large metal bowl and the mixer's wire whisk attachment for at least 30 minutes prior to making the whipped cream.

3. To make the cake, use an electric mixer to beat the egg whites on high speed until stiff peaks form.

4. In a separate bowl (by hand or with an electric mixer), combine the entire soaked farina mixture (including any remaining milk) with the egg yolks, sugar, walnuts, baking powder, flour, and vanilla extract until well mixed. Gently fold in the egg whites by hand, taking care not to knock the air out of the whites.

5. Divide the batter evenly between the two cake pans; bake for 25 to 35 minutes, until a cake tester inserted in the middle comes out clean. Transfer to a wire cooling rack; cool in the pans for 10 to 15 minutes, then turn out the layers onto the rack to cool completely before adding toppings.

6. Using the chilled bowl and an electric mixer with the whisk attachment, whip the cream on high speed until soft peaks are just about to form, 1 to 2 minutes; add the vanilla extract and powdered sugar and continue beating until stiff peaks form, 4 to 5 minutes.

7. Spread the whipped cream on top of the first layer; cover with mandarin orange slices. Place the second layer on top of the first, then spread whipped cream on top; layer with remaining mandarin orange slices. Refrigerate if not served immediately.

Note: Farina and Cream of Wheat are very similar. Both are made from wheat, but Cream of Wheat is a specific brand of farina. It has a finer texture than traditional farina and is available in different flavors. I used generic farina in this recipe and have not tried preparing it with Cream of Wheat. Farina actually comes from semolina, which is the "middlings" of milled wheat; it has been used in Jewish cooking since ancient times.

Icebox Cake

This cake tastes like a cross between a Baked Alaska and a gelatin icebox cake, which was popular at the time. I made this with strawberry gelatin and sliced strawberries, but you can use any combination of flavored gelatin and fruit that suits your taste.

Ingredients

Filling:

2 cups set gelatin, any flavor (3-ounce box)

2 cups sliced fruit of choice

1½ cups whipped cream (recipe below, or substitute 1½ cups Cool Whip)

Crust:

2 cups crushed cookies (see note)

¼ cup (½ stick) salted butter, melted

Whipped Cream:

1 cup heavy whipping cream, very cold

1 teaspoon vanilla extract

1 to 2 tablespoons powdered sugar, sifted

Meringue:

6 large egg whites, room temperature

½ teaspoon cream of tartar

⅓ cup granulated sugar

Pinch of salt

1 teaspoon vanilla extract

Plan ahead

1. Make your preferred flavor of gelatin ahead of time according to the package directions and allow it to set completely. For best results if opting for homemade whipped cream, chill a metal bowl and the wire whisk attachment for the mixer for at least 30 minutes before using. Once the crust is filled, the fruit mixture will need to freeze overnight or at least for several hours, so plan accordingly.

Directions

2. Preheat the oven to 350 degrees. Grease the bottom and sides of an 8- or 9-inch pie pan.

3. To make the crust, combine the crushed cookies and melted butter; line the bottom and sides of the pie pan with the cookie mixture. Bake for 10 minutes, until the crust is just set.

4. Prepare the whipped cream if not using Cool Whip. Using the chilled bowl and whisk attachment, whip the cream with an electric mixer on high speed until soft peaks are just about to form, 1 to 2 minutes; add the vanilla extract and powdered sugar and continue beating on high until stiff peaks form, 4 to 5 minutes.

5. To prepare the filling, run a fork through the set gelatin several times until you have small pieces; combine the gelatin pieces with the whipped cream and fruit. Fill the cookie crust with the fruit/whipped cream mixture; freeze until firm, overnight or at least 2 to 3 hours.

6. When the filling in the freezer is firm, prepare the meringue; preheat the oven to 450 degrees if you will be using the oven (rather than a kitchen torch) to toast the meringue.

7. To make the meringue, use an electric mixer with a whisk attachment to beat the egg whites and cream of tartar on medium speed for 1 minute; increase to high speed until soft peaks form, about 4 more minutes. Add the sugar, salt, and vanilla extract; continue beating on high speed until glossy, stiff peaks form, about 2 more minutes.

8. Remove the pie pan from the freezer. Spread the meringue on top of the filling using a large spoon or a pastry bag fitted with a large open star tip to pipe swirls of meringue, extending it to the edges to completely cover the filling.

9. To bake the meringue, use either a kitchen torch or the oven. If using a kitchen torch, toast the entire meringue topping. If using the oven, bake at 450 degrees for 4 to 5 minutes, until the meringue is just toasted. *Do not overbake*, as the filling will melt.

10. Slice and serve immediately. Refrigerate any remaining portion.

Note for crushed cookies: The original recipe called for macaroon snaps. I had a hard time finding these, so I used Lorna Doone Shortbread Cookies. You can also use vanilla wafers, animal crackers, graham crackers, or any similar cookie.

Note for meringue: Egg whites must be at room temperature for the best, fluffiest meringue.

(Not So) Plain Loaf Cake

I renamed this recipe because the taste is anything but plain. It is a simple but versatile cake recipe; enjoy variations by replacing the vanilla or lemon extract with almost any extract you prefer. Mix in nuts, raisins, or chocolate chips. Serve it plain, with whipped cream, or with a fruit topping. For this version, I decided to go with a cream cheese glaze, raspberries, and powdered sugar.

Ingredients

Cake:

2 cups cake flour, sifted

1½ teaspoons baking powder

Pinch of salt

½ cup (1 stick) unsalted butter, room temperature

1 cup granulated sugar

2 large eggs, well beaten, room temperature

1 teaspoon vanilla or lemon extract

¾ cup whole milk, room temperature

Nuts, raisins, or chocolate chips (optional)

Raspberries (optional garnish)

Powdered sugar (optional garnish)

Cream Cheese Glaze:

8 ounces full-fat cream cheese, room temperature

2 cups powdered sugar, sifted

¼ cup whole milk or heavy cream, room temperature

1 teaspoon vanilla extract

Directions

1. Preheat the oven to 350 degrees. Grease the sides of a standard 8 cup loaf pan and line the bottom with parchment paper. Sift together the cake flour, baking powder, and salt; set aside.

2. Using an electric mixer on medium speed, cream the butter and sugar until light and fluffy, about 2 to 3 minutes; add the beaten eggs and vanilla extract.

3. Alternate adding the sifted flour mixture and the milk until all ingredients are incorporated, taking care not to overmix the batter. Stop the mixer and scrape down the sides of the bowl with a spatula to make sure all ingredients are incorporated. Mix in nuts, raisins, chocolate chips, or other additions, if desired.

4. Pour the batter into the prepared loaf pan; bake for 30 to 40 minutes, until a cake tester inserted in the middle of the cake comes out clean. Transfer to a wire cooling rack to cool completely in the pan, then turn out the loaf before serving. Serve plain, sliced and toasted, or with toppings of your choice.

5. To make a cream cheese glaze, combine the cream cheese, powdered sugar, milk, and vanilla extract in a small bowl; mix by hand or with an electric mixer until smooth. Add more milk if you need a thinner consistency. Drizzle the icing over the cooled cake; garnish with raspberries or other fruit and dust with powdered sugar, if desired.

Poppy Seed Cake

If you like poppy seed muffins, you'll love this cake version. Although the original recipe is delicious as a plain cake, I also enjoy it paired with a lemon cream cheese glaze and garnished with fresh berries. Did someone say they want seconds?

Ingredients

Cake:

½ cup poppy seeds, soaked overnight

¾ cup whole milk, room temperature

2 cups cake flour, sifted

2 teaspoons baking powder

4 large egg whites, room temperature

½ cup (1 stick) unsalted butter, room temperature

1 cup granulated sugar

1 lemon, zest and juice (2 to 3 tablespoons)

Fresh blueberries, strawberries, or raspberries (optional garnish)

Lemon Cream Cheese Glaze:

3 ounces full-fat cream cheese, room temperature

1½ cups powdered sugar, sifted

1 teaspoon lemon zest

1 tablespoon fresh lemon juice

½ teaspoon vanilla extract

Plan ahead

1. Combine the poppy seeds and milk; soak overnight in the refrigerator. Allow all ingredients to come to room temperature. **Tip:** Room temperature egg whites beat up fluffier than cold egg whites.

Directions

2. Preheat the oven to 350 degrees. Liberally grease a 10-inch (10- to 12-cup) Bundt pan and dust with flour; tap the pan to remove excess flour. Sift together the cake flour and baking powder; set aside.

3. Using an electric mixer with a whisk attachment, beat the egg whites on high speed until stiff peaks form, 4 to 5 minutes.

4. In a separate bowl, use an electric mixer with a paddle attachment to cream the butter and sugar until light and fluffy, 2 to 3 minutes. While continuing to mix, alternate adding the sifted flour mixture and the entire poppy seed mixture (including any remaining milk). Add the zest and juice of 1 lemon. Stop the mixer and gently fold in the beaten egg whites by hand, taking care not to knock the air out of the whites.

5. Pour the batter into the prepared pan; bake for 45 to 55 minutes, until a cake tester inserted in the middle comes out clean. Transfer to a wire cooling rack; cool in the pan for 10 to 15 minutes before inverting the cake onto the rack. Remove the pan and allow the cake to cool completely before adding the glaze.

6. For the lemon cream cheese glaze, beat the cream cheese with an electric mixer until fluffy, 2 to 3 minutes. Slowly add the powdered sugar, lemon zest, lemon juice, and vanilla extract. Stop the mixer and scrape down the sides of the bowl to make sure all ingredients are well incorporated, and adjust the amount of lemon juice to the desired consistency for icing. Drizzle the glaze over the cooled cake using a fork. Garnish the cake with fresh berries.

Prince of Vale Cake

While the original recipe limited its flavorings to cinnamon and currants, I added brown sugar, dates, and chopped Brazil nuts to further the Kashmiri theme of this cake. Serve this plain, dusted with powdered sugar, or drizzled with cinnamon cream cheese icing.

Ingredients

Cake:

2 cups cake flour, sifted

1 teaspoon ground cinnamon

1 teaspoon baking soda

1 teaspoon baking powder

½ cup (1 stick) unsalted butter, room temperature

1 cup granulated sugar

½ cup light or dark brown sugar, lightly packed

1 teaspoon vanilla extract

2 large eggs, well beaten, room temperature

1 cup sour milk (see note) or buttermilk, room temperature

⅔ cup currants or raisins

1 cup chopped Brazil nuts

1 cup chopped pitted dates

Cinnamon Cream Cheese Icing:

8 ounces full-fat cream cheese, room temperature

½ cup (1 stick) unsalted butter, room temperature

1 teaspoon vanilla extract

½ to 1 tablespoon ground cinnamon (more to taste)

2 cups powdered sugar, sifted

Directions

1. Preheat the oven to 350 degrees. Liberally grease a 10-inch (10- to 12-cup) Bundt pan and dust with flour; tap the inverted pan to remove excess flour. Sift together the cake flour, cinnamon, baking soda, and baking powder; set aside.

2. With an electric mixer, cream the butter, granulated sugar, and brown sugar on medium speed until light and fluffy, 2 to 3 minutes. Add the vanilla extract, then the beaten eggs; the mixture should appear light and creamy. Alternate adding the sifted flour mixture and the sour milk, a little at a time. Add the currants, chopped Brazil nuts, and chopped dates. Continue to beat on medium speed until the ingredients are just combined; do not overbeat. Stop the mixer, scrape down the sides of the bowl with a spatula, and gently finish incorporating the ingredients by hand with a spatula.

3. Pour the batter into the prepared pan; bake for 45 to 55 minutes, until a cake tester inserted in the middle comes out clean. Transfer to a wire cooling rack; cool in the pan for 10 to 15 minutes before inverting the cake onto the rack. Remove the pan and allow the cake to cool completely.

4. To make the cinnamon cream cheese icing, use an electric mixer to cream the cream cheese and butter on medium speed until light and fluffy, 2 to 3 minutes; add the vanilla extract and cinnamon. Decrease the mixer to slow speed and add the powdered sugar ½ cup at a time. Thin the mixture with water, milk, or heavy cream to the desired consistency. Using a spoon or fork, drizzle the icing over the cooled cake.

Note: To replicate sour milk, add 1 tablespoon white vinegar or lemon juice to 1 cup whole milk; allow it to stand for at least 5 minutes before using. Buttermilk can be substituted (omit the vinegar or lemon juice) and will give a slightly richer texture.

I have no idea why this cake was named "Prince of Vale." An internet search revealed no such notable historic figure. However, I did run across a luxurious vacation destination: the Prince of Vale houseboat in Kashmir, known for its gourmet Kashmiri dishes.

The original recipe used cinnamon and currants as its flavorings: Not too exotic for today's recipes, but perhaps they inspired the author to dream of a vacation in a faraway land once the Great Depression was over.

By the way, you can still book an exotic vacation on the Prince of Vale houseboat in Srinagar!

Ripple Cake

Crumb cake . . . but the crumbs are in the cake! Top with old-fashioned browned-butter icing and you have a scrumptious cake that will impress anyone who tries it.

Ingredients

Cake:

2 cups cake flour, sifted

2 teaspoons baking powder

½ cup (1 stick) unsalted butter, room temperature

½ cup granulated sugar

½ cup light brown sugar, lightly packed

2 large eggs, well beaten, room temperature

1 cup whole milk, room temperature

1 teaspoon vanilla extract

Browned-Butter Icing:

6 tablespoons unsalted butter, room temperature

2 cups powdered sugar, sifted

1 teaspoon ground cinnamon

Pinch of salt

1 teaspoon vanilla extract

4 to 6 tablespoons heavy cream

Chopped pecans (optional)

Directions

1. Preheat the oven to 350 degrees. Liberally grease a 10-inch (10- to 12-cup) Bundt pan and dust with flour; tap the inverted pan to remove excess flour. Sift together the cake flour and baking powder; set aside.

2. Using an electric mixer with a paddle attachment, cream the butter, granulated sugar, and brown sugar on medium speed until light and fluffy, 2 to 3 minutes. Add the sifted flour mixture and mix until it has a crumb-like texture. Reserve ½ cup crumb mixture to add in separately.

3. Combine the remaining crumb mixture with the eggs, milk, and vanilla extract until it reaches a smooth consistency. Fold in the reserved crumb mixture.

4. Pour the batter into the prepared pan; bake for 45 to 55 minutes, until a cake tester inserted in the middle of the cake comes out clean. Transfer to a wire cooling rack; cool in the pan for 10 to 15 minutes before inverting the cake onto the rack. Remove the pan and allow the cake to cool completely before icing or dusting with powdered sugar.

5. To make the browned-butter icing, melt the butter in a skillet over medium heat. Allow the butter to brown, making sure to continually move the skillet over the heat so as not to burn the butter. When the melted butter is golden brown with some dark specks, remove from the heat and allow the butter to cool until just warm to the touch, 10 to 15 minutes.

6. In a separate bowl, sift together the powdered sugar, cinnamon, and salt. With an electric mixer on medium speed, combine the powdered sugar mixture and browned butter until well combined. Add the vanilla extract, then add the heavy cream 2 tablespoons at a time until the mixture reaches the desired consistency. Drizzle the icing over the cooled cake; top with chopped pecans, if desired.

Variations: Add ½ to 1 cup chopped nuts or 1 teaspoon cinnamon (or both) after adding the flour mixture.

Banana Devil's Food Cake

This light, extra-moist chocolate cake has a banana custard filling added in the middle before baking—it's a unique cake you'll bake again. The trick with this cake is to evenly divide the amount of cake batter between the two layers. I have had the best results when using an 8-inch springform pan.

Ingredients

Filling:

1 cup granulated sugar

1 cup whole milk, room temperature

1 tablespoon all-purpose flour

3 large egg yolks, room temperature

3 ripe bananas, mashed

½ cup chopped pitted dates

½ cup chopped walnuts

Cake:

2 cups cake flour, sifted

1 teaspoon baking soda

Pinch of salt

½ cup (1 stick) unsalted butter, room temperature

1 cup granulated sugar

1 large egg, well beaten, room temperature

1 teaspoon vanilla extract

1 ounce (28 g) semisweet chocolate baking bar, melted

1 cup sour milk (see note) or buttermilk, room temperature

Chocolate Cream Cheese Icing:

3½ cups powdered sugar, sifted

⅔ cup unsweetened cocoa powder, sifted

Pinch of salt

12 ounces full-fat cream cheese, room temperature

¾ cup (1½ sticks) unsalted butter, room temperature

1 teaspoon vanilla extract

1 to 2 tablespoons whole milk or heavy cream, room temperature

Directions

1. Prepare the filling first so that it can cool slightly while you make the cake batter. In a small saucepan over medium heat, combine the sugar, milk, all-purpose flour, and egg yolks. Bring the mixture to a slow boil, stirring constantly to prevent it from sticking to the bottom of the saucepan.

2. Continue cooking until thickened to a pudding-like consistency; remove from the heat. Add the banana, dates, and walnuts. Stir well to thoroughly combine. Set aside the filling to cool while making the cake batter.

3. Preheat the oven to 350 degrees. Prepare an 8- or 9-inch springform pan (no larger) by greasing the sides of the pan and lining the bottom with parchment paper. Sift together the cake flour, baking soda, and salt; set aside.

4. In a separate bowl, use an electric mixer with a paddle attachment to cream the butter and sugar on medium speed until light and fluffy, 2 to 3 minutes. Add the beaten egg, vanilla extract, and melted chocolate; continue mixing. Alternate adding the sifted flour mixture and the sour milk. Alternate adding the flour mixture and the milk, then stop the mixer and scrape down the sides of the bowl with a spatula to make sure all ingredients are thoroughly combined. Finish mixing by hand to avoid overmixing the batter. You should have about 5 cups of batter.

5. Pour exactly half of the cake batter into the prepared pan. Add the filling on top, spreading it out evenly. Spoon in the remainder of the batter on top, making sure all the filling is covered.

6. Bake for 45 to 55 minutes, until a cake tester inserted in the middle comes out clean. Transfer to a wire cooling rack; cool in the pan for 10 to 15 minutes. Remove the collar after the initial cooling; allow the cake to cool completely before icing. This cake is good enough to stand alone (or with a dusting of powdered sugar), or you can cover it with chocolate cream cheese icing.

7. To prepare the chocolate cream cheese icing, first sift together the powdered sugar, cocoa powder, and salt; set aside. Using an electric mixer on high speed, beat the cream cheese and butter until smooth and creamy, about 1 minute. Slowly add the sifted powdered sugar mixture, vanilla extract, and milk until thoroughly combined. Add more milk if needed to obtain the desired icing consistency. Spread the icing over the cooled cake.

Note: This is one cake that you will need to test frequently for doneness. It may take longer than the stated time depending on your oven. Be patient! The results are worth it.

Note: To replicate sour milk, add 1 tablespoon white vinegar or lemon juice to 1 cup whole milk; allow it to stand for at least 5 minutes before using. Buttermilk can be substituted (omit the vinegar or lemon juice) and will give a slightly richer texture. The original recipe calls for sour milk. In the days of the Great Depression, nothing was wasted, so a cake was a good way to use up old or sour milk. In the spirit of the original recipes, I mainly use replicated sour milk.

Shortcake

A classic favorite, the traditional shortcake is more like a biscuit than a cake. It's most often topped with strawberries, but many fruits can be used: almost any berry, peaches, or even cooked apples. Dust with powdered sugar or serve with homemade whipped cream—or both. Yum!

Ingredients

Shortcake:

1 cup all-purpose flour, sifted

1 tablespoon baking powder

¼ cup (½ stick) *cold* butter, cut into small pieces

2 large eggs, well beaten, room temperature

1 cup granulated sugar

1 teaspoon vanilla extract

Pinch of salt

½ cup whole milk, room temperature

1 to 2 cups berries, peaches, or cooked apples

Whipped Cream Topping:

1 cup heavy whipping cream, very cold

1 teaspoon vanilla extract (see variation below)

1 to 2 tablespoons powdered sugar, sifted

Directions

1. Preheat the oven to 350 degrees. Grease the sides of one 8- or 9-inch layer pan and line the bottom with parchment paper.

2. To make the shortcake, sift together the flour and baking powder; cut in the cold butter with a pastry blender or your fingers until the mixture resembles small crumbs.

3. In a separate bowl with an electric mixer on medium speed, cream the eggs and sugar, about 2 to 3 minutes. Add the vanilla extract and the salt. Continue mixing; alternate adding the crumbled flour mixture and the milk until all ingredients are incorporated.

4. Spread the batter in the prepared pan; bake for 25 to 35 minutes, until a cake tester inserted in the middle of the shortcake comes out clean. While the shortcake is baking, chill a metal bowl and whisk attachment for the mixer so that they will be ready when making the whipped cream topping.

5. Transfer the layer pan to a wire cooling rack; leave the cake to cool in the pan for 10 to 15 minutes before turning it out onto the rack. While the cake is still warm, use a serrated knife to carefully cut the cake horizontally into two even layers. Let the sliced layers cool completely.

6. To prepare the whipped cream topping, chill both a metal bowl and wire whisk attachment for at least 30 minutes prior to using. Whip the cream with an electric mixer on high speed until soft peaks are just about to form, 1 to 2 minutes; add the vanilla extract and powdered sugar and continue beating on high until stiff peaks form, 4 to 5 minutes.

7. To assemble the shortcake, top the first cake layer with berries or other fresh fruit and whipped cream. Place the second cake layer on top; add more fruit and whipped cream.

Variation: When preparing the whipped cream topping, substitute the vanilla with almost any extract of your choice, such as almond or strawberry.

"Short" Trivia

Shortcake recipes date back to England in the late 1500s. Later "strawberry cakes" were made with unleavened dough (no raising agent). Leave it to the Americans to add baking soda or baking powder, which gave it a biscuit-like texture. By the 1850s, strawberry shortcake had become a popular American dessert—so popular, in fact, that June 14 is National Strawberry Shortcake Day in the United States!

The original Shortcake recipe calls for 4 tablespoons of baking powder. I would *not* recommend it!

Eggless-Butterless-Milkless Cake

Despite the "lessness" of the ingredients, this cake is quite delicious even if you don't need to ration your supplies. The taste and texture remind me of a spiced bread pudding. Serve plain, dust with powdered sugar, or top with cinnamon cream cheese icing. Bonus: You don't even have to break out the mixer for this one!

Ingredients

Cake:

½ teaspoon baking soda

1 tablespoon water

¼ cup vegetable shortening

1 cup granulated sugar

2 cups raisins

1 cup water

1 teaspoon ground cinnamon

½ teaspoon ground cloves

½ teaspoon salt

2 cups cake flour, sifted

1 cup chopped walnuts

Cinnamon Cream Cheese Icing:

8 ounces full-fat cream cheese, room temperature

2 cups powdered sugar, sifted

¼ cup whole milk or heavy cream, room temperature

1 teaspoon vanilla extract

½ teaspoon ground cinnamon

Directions

1. Preheat the oven to 350 degrees. Grease the sides of a 9- or 10-inch springform pan and line the bottom with parchment paper. Dissolve the baking soda in 1 tablespoon water; set aside.

2. Combine the shortening, sugar, raisins, 1 cup water, cinnamon, cloves, and salt in a saucepan; bring to a boil and continue boiling for 3 minutes. Remove from the heat. Add the dissolved baking soda mixture, flour, and walnuts; mix well with a spatula until all ingredients are thoroughly combined.

3. Pour the batter into the prepared pan; bake at 350 degrees for 35 to 40 minutes, until a cake tester inserted in the middle comes out clean. Transfer to a wire cooling rack; cool in the pan for 10 to 15 minutes before removing the collar of the springform pan.

4. To make the cinnamon cream cheese icing, use an electric mixer on medium speed to combine the cream cheese, powdered sugar, milk, vanilla extract, and cinnamon until smooth; add extra cinnamon, if desired. For a thinner consistency, add more milk; to thicken, add more powdered sugar. Drizzle the icing over the cooled cake.

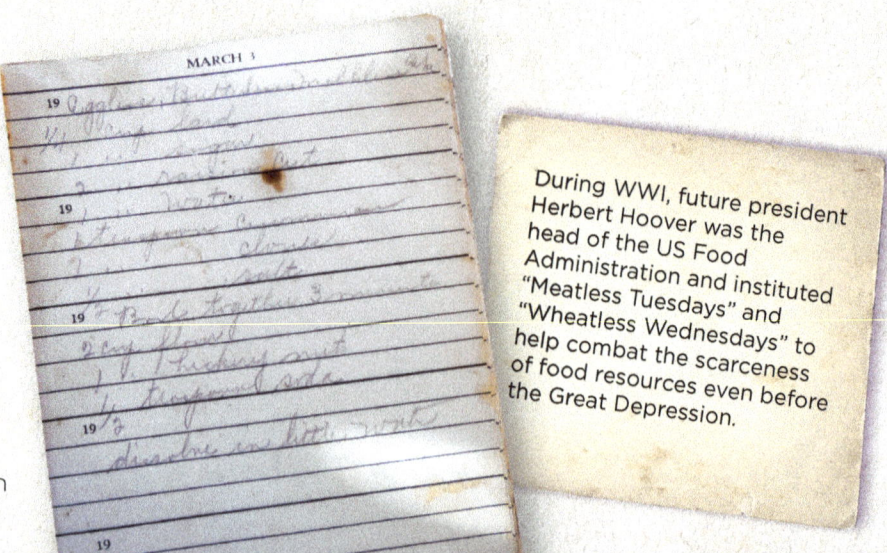

During WWI, future president Herbert Hoover was the head of the US Food Administration and instituted "Meatless Tuesdays" and "Wheatless Wednesdays" to help combat the scarceness of food resources even before the Great Depression.

Apple Shortcake

This very moist cake has an old-fashioned appeal. Serve plain or top with a brown sugar glaze or whipped cream.

Ingredients

Cake:

2 cups cake flour, sifted

1 teaspoon baking powder

1 teaspoon ground cinnamon (optional)

Pinch of salt

½ cup (1 stick) unsalted butter, melted

1 cup granulated sugar

1 teaspoon vanilla extract

1 large egg, well beaten, room temperature

½ cup applesauce

1 cup whole milk, room temperature

Brown Sugar Glaze:

¼ cup (½ stick) unsalted butter, room temperature

½ cup light or dark brown sugar, lightly packed

2 tablespoons whole milk or heavy cream, room temperature

2 cups powdered sugar, sifted

¼ teaspoon vanilla extract

¼ cup toasted chopped nuts (optional)

Directions

1. Preheat the oven to 350 degrees. Liberally grease a 10-inch (10- to 12-cup) Bundt pan and dust with flour; tap the inverted pan to remove excess flour. Sift together the cake flour, baking powder, optional cinnamon, and salt; set aside.

2. Using an electric mixer with a paddle attachment, cream the butter and sugar on medium speed until light and fluffy, 2 to 3 minutes. Add the vanilla extract and beaten egg, then the applesauce. Alternate adding the flour mixture and the milk until all ingredients are incorporated. Stop the mixer and scrape down the sides of the bowl with a spatula to make sure all ingredients are well incorporated; finish mixing by hand to avoid overmixing.

3. Pour the batter into the prepared pan; bake for 45 to 55 minutes, until a cake tester inserted in the middle comes out clean. Transfer to a wire cooling rack; cool in the pan for 10 to 15 minutes before inverting the cake onto the rack. Remove the pan and allow the cake to cool completely.

4. To make the brown sugar glaze, combine the butter, brown sugar, and milk in a saucepan over medium heat. Stir constantly until the sugar has melted; remove from the heat. Add the powdered sugar until the desired consistency is reached, then add the vanilla extract. Add more powdered sugar for a thicker consistency or more milk for a thinner consistency. Drizzle the glaze over the cooled cake; sprinkle with toasted chopped nuts, if desired.

Orange Supreme Cake

This chiffon-type cake is super moist with a hint of orange—or you can add more to suit your tastes. Topped with orange supreme icing, it reminds me of an old-fashioned Creamsicle® bar, that frozen childhood treat. By the way, National Creamsicle® Day is August 14!

Ingredients

Cake:

2 cups cake flour, sifted

½ teaspoon baking powder

Pinch of salt

4 large eggs, separated, room temperature

1 medium orange, juice (⅓ cup) and zest

½ cup water

½ cup (1 stick) unsalted butter, room temperature

2 cups granulated sugar

1 teaspoon orange extract (optional)

Orange Supreme Icing:

8 ounces full-fat cream cheese, room temperature

¼ cup (½ stick) unsalted butter, room temperature

1 teaspoon orange extract

1½ teaspoon orange zest (optional)

Pinch of salt

1 cup powdered sugar, sifted

¼ cup whole milk or heavy cream, room temperature

Orange slices (optional garnish)

Directions

1. Preheat the oven to 350 degrees. Prepare a 10-inch (10- to 12-cup) Bundt pan or two 8- or 9-inch layer pans. If using a Bundt pan, liberally grease the pan and dust with flour; tap the inverted pan to remove excess flour. Or if using layer cake pans, grease the sides of the pans and line the bottoms with parchment paper.

2. Sift together the cake flour, baking powder, and salt; set aside. Separate the eggs. Beat the egg yolks and set aside. The egg whites should remain at room temperature until needed later. Combine the orange juice, orange zest, and water; set aside.

3. Using an electric mixer with a paddle attachment, cream the butter and sugar on medium speed until light and fluffy, 2 to 3 minutes. Add the beaten egg yolks to the butter mixture; mix well. Add the optional orange extract, if using. Alternate adding the sifted flour mixture and the orange juice mixture. Stop the mixer and scrape down the sides of the bowl with a spatula to make sure all ingredients are well incorporated; finish mixing by hand to avoid overmixing.

4. In a separate bowl, use an electric mixer with a whisk attachment to beat the egg whites on high speed until soft peaks form; gently fold the egg whites into the butter mixture.

5. Pour the batter into the prepared pan(s); bake for 45 to 55 minutes for a Bundt pan or 25 to 35 minutes for layer pans, until a cake tester inserted in the middle comes out clean. Transfer to a wire cooling rack; cool in the pan(s) for 10 to 15 minutes. Then for a Bundt pan, invert the cake onto the rack; remove the pan. For layer cake pans, turn out the cakes onto the rack. Cool completely before icing.

6. To prepare the orange supreme icing, use an electric mixer to beat the cream cheese and butter on medium speed until light and fluffy, 2 to 3 minutes. Beat in the orange extract, optional orange zest, and salt. Add the powdered sugar 1 tablespoon at a time and beat to combine; stop the mixer at intervals to scrape the sides of the bowl and incorporate all ingredients.

7. Add the milk 1 tablespoon at a time, beating it into the cream cheese mixture until combined. (Add less milk for a thicker consistency or more milk for a thinner consistency.) Pour the icing over the cooled cake, and garnish with sliced oranges if desired.

Holland Rusk Cake

This is absolutely scrumptious! Holland rusk is a light, sweet toast. For this recipe, it's been crushed to a texture like graham cracker crumbs and mixed with sugar and butter to make the crust for this cake. The filling is a rich, creamy custard, and it's topped with a wonderful meringue. True confession: The first time I made this, I ate the whole thing by myself!

Ingredients

Crust:

½ cup (1 stick) salted butter, melted

½ cup granulated sugar

3.5-ounce package Holland rusk toast, crushed fine (see note)

Custard Filling:

2 large egg yolks, room temperature

2 tablespoons granulated sugar

¾ cup (1½ sticks) unsalted butter, room temperature

2 cups whole milk, room temperature

1 teaspoon vanilla extract

2 tablespoons cornstarch

Meringue Topping:

6 large egg whites, room temperature

½ teaspoon cream of tartar

⅓ cup granulated sugar

1 teaspoon vanilla

Pinch of salt

Directions

1. Preheat the oven to 325 degrees. Grease the sides of a 9- or 10-inch springform pan and line the bottom with parchment paper.

2. To make the crust, combine the melted butter, sugar, and Holland rusk crumbs until thoroughly mixed. Press the mixture on the bottom and up the sides of the springform pan. Prebake the crust for 10 minutes.

3. While the crust is baking, make the custard filling. Combine the egg yolks, sugar, butter and milk in a saucepan and cook over medium-high heat, stirring constantly. Sift in the cornstarch using a cake sifter or a tea strainer to prevent the starch from clumping. Do not allow to boil. Remove from the heat once the mixture has thickened to a pudding-like consistency, approximately 8 to 10 minutes. Stir in the vanilla extract.

4. Make the meringue using room-temperature egg whites; the oven should remain at 325 degrees. Using an electric mixer with a whisk attachment, beat the egg whites and cream of tartar on medium speed for 1 minute; increase to high speed until soft peaks form, about 4 more minutes. Add the sugar, vanilla, and salt; continue beating on high speed until glossy, stiff peaks form, about 2 more minutes.

5. Pour the filling into the crust. Spread or pipe the meringue on top, extending it to the edges to completely cover the filling. Bake for 15 to 20 minutes, until the meringue begins to turn golden brown. Transfer to a wire cooling rack; cool in the pan for 10 to 15 minutes before removing the collar of the springform pan. Cool completely before serving.

What Is Holland Rusk?

I had never heard of Holland rusk before making the Holland Rusk Cake.

Beschuit, or Holland rusk (or simply rusk), is a twice-baked bread popular in many parts of the world. Rusk can be traced back to South Africa as long ago as 1690. Twice baking the bread was a way to preserve it, and it was often packed when traveling long distances. In Holland, rusk topped with either pink or blue sprinkles is still served when celebrating a newborn. It is very popular in India as a tea toast, and a chocolate-topped version is enjoyed in Japan.

Rusk is a bit like biscotti, which means "twice baked" in Italian. The difference is rusk is more of a twice-baked cake, whereas biscotti is a twice-baked cookie.

Where do you find Holland rusk? Not a lot of American grocery stores routinely carry it; markets that specialize in European food will sometimes have it. You can easily find it online, and if all else fails, recipes for rusk can be found online as well.

Cheese Torte

A bit denser than cheesecake (but easier to make), this torte has a sweet, crispy crust made from Holland rusk toast. For a really scrumptious treat, serve with fruit, whipped cream, or both.

Ingredients

Crust:

3.5-ounce package Holland rusk toast, crushed fine (see note)

3 tablespoons unsalted butter, melted

½ cup granulated sugar

1 large egg, well beaten, room temperature

Filling:

4 large eggs, well beaten, room temperature

1½ cups granulated sugar

¼ cup all-purpose flour, sifted

1 cup heavy whipping cream, room temperature

Strawberries, blueberries, or peaches (optional garnish)

Whipped Cream Topping:

1 cup heavy whipping cream, very cold

1 teaspoon vanilla extract

1 to 2 tablespoons powdered sugar, sifted

Plan Ahead

1. To make the crust, preheat the oven to 350 degrees.

2. Combine the rusk crumbs, butter, sugar, and egg in a large bowl; mix well. Press into the bottom and up the sides of an 8- or 9-inch pie pan.

3. Bake for 8 to 10 minutes, until just barely browned; allow to cool completely before adding the filling.

4. If making whipped cream, for best results chill a metal bowl and a wire whisk attachment for the mixer.

Directions

5. Before making the filling, preheat the oven to 350 degrees.

6. Using an electric mixer on medium speed, beat together the eggs and sugar until light in color and slightly frothy, 2 to 3 minutes. Add the flour and cream; mix until the ingredients are just combined (do not overmix).

7. Pour the filling into the cooled crust; bake for 30 minutes, until a cake tester inserted in the middle comes out clean. Serve with fruit or whipped cream, if desired.

8. If making the whipped cream topping: Chill both a metal bowl and wire whisk attachment for at least 30 minutes prior to using. In a large bowl, whip the cream with an electric mixer on high speed until soft peaks are just about to form, 1 to 2 minutes; add the vanilla extract and powdered sugar and continue beating on high until stiff peaks form, 4 to 5 minutes.

9. Spread the whipped cream over the cooled pie. Refrigerate if not serving immediately.

Note: I order Holland rusk online from Amazon.

Note for whipped cream: Recipe may be doubled or tripled as desired. Other extract flavors may be substituted for the vanilla.

Royal Fruit Cake

"Yuck! Fruit cake!" But actually, this is pretty darn good. There's more "cake" than "fruit" in this, which makes it much lighter than the traditional fruit cakes that folks (try to) serve at Christmas. Give this one a taste!

Ingredients

2 cups cake flour, sifted

1 teaspoon baking soda

1 teaspoon cream of tartar

1 teaspoon ground cinnamon

¼ teaspoon ground nutmeg

1 cup currants or raisins

1 cup pecans, chopped fine

½ cup diced candied citron (see note)

1 cup (2 sticks) unsalted butter, room temperature

2 cups light or dark brown sugar, lightly packed

3 large eggs, well beaten, room temperature

1 teaspoon vanilla extract

1 cup whole milk, room temperature

Powdered sugar (optional topping)

1 cup apricot preserves (optional topping)

Directions

1. Preheat the oven to 350 degrees. Liberally grease a 10-inch (10- to 12-cup) Bundt pan and dust with flour; tap the inverted pan to remove excess flour. Sift together the cake flour, baking soda, cream of tartar, cinnamon, and nutmeg; add the currants, pecans, and citron. Mix well and set aside.

2. Using an electric mixer with a paddle attachment, cream the butter and brown sugar on medium speed until light and fluffy, 2 to 3 minutes. Add the beaten eggs and vanilla extract. Alternate adding the flour mixture and the milk; stop the mixer and scrape the sides of the bowl with a spatula until all ingredients are well incorporated. Finish mixing by hand to avoid overmixing.

3. Pour the batter into the prepared pan; bake for 45 to 55 minutes, until a cake tester inserted in the middle comes out clean. Transfer to a wire cooling rack; cool in the pan for 10 to 15 minutes before inverting the cake onto the rack. Remove the pan and allow the cake to cool completely if topping with powdered sugar.

4. Dust with powdered sugar, or spread warm apricot preserves over the cake.

Note: Candied citron can often be found in grocery stores around the holidays, but it can be ordered online year-round.

Schammon Torte

More commonly known as a schaum torte, this dessert is the German version of pavlova. According to my research, this dessert is not well known by this name outside of Wisconsin, which gives credence to the theory that the cookbook was originally found in an estate sale somewhere in northwest Wisconsin.

Ingredients

Torte:

6 large egg whites, room temperature

Pinch of salt

Pinch of cream of tartar

2 cups granulated sugar

1 teaspoon vanilla extract

Fresh fruit (optional filling)

Custard Filling:

1 to 2 tablespoons cornstarch

¾ cup granulated sugar

Pinch of salt

2 cups whole milk, room temperature

2 large egg yolks, well beaten, room temperature

1 teaspoon vanilla extract

Whipped Cream Filling:

1 cup heavy whipping cream, very cold

1 teaspoon vanilla extract

1 to 2 tablespoons powdered sugar, sifted

Plan Ahead

1. For best results, egg whites must be at room temperature for the best, fluffiest meringue. Choose your preferred type of filling (custard, whipped cream, fruit, or ice cream). If making the whipped cream filling, chill a metal bowl and wire whisk attachment for the mixer at least 30 minutes prior to using.

Directions

2. Preheat the oven to 250 degrees. Size a piece of parchment paper to fit a sheet pan, then use a permanent marker or pen to draw a circle on the parchment in the diameter you want your torte to be. You can make one large or several individual tortes. Flip the parchment over in the pan (markings facing down) to line the sheet pan.

3. Using an electric mixer with a whisk attachment, beat the egg whites, salt, and cream of tartar until soft peaks form, 4 to 5 minutes. Add the sugar and vanilla extract very slowly and continue to beat on high until stiff peaks form, 3 to 4 minutes.

4. Spread the meringue mixture with a large spoon on the prepared parchment, or pipe more precisely with a pastry bag and a star tip. If using a spoon, drop large spoonfuls of meringue onto your outlined circles; use the back side of the spoon to make a hollow in the middle (there should still be meringue at the bottom of the "well"). If using a piping bag, pipe a filled circle, smooth with a spoon, and then pipe 1 to 2 layers of meringue on top of the base circle to form a "wall."

5. Bake the meringue shells for 1 hour; turn off the heat and leave the shells in the closed oven for another 30 minutes.

6. When the shells are completely cool, fill with custard, whipped cream, fruit, or ice cream—or any combination of those.

7. **For the custard filling:** While the meringue shells are baking, make the custard filling, if desired. Combine the flour, sugar, and salt; set aside.

8. In a small saucepan, heat the milk on medium-high, stirring constantly. Do not allow mixture to boil. Cook until thickened, 4 to 5 minutes. Gradually add the beaten egg yolks into the hot milk mixture, about 1 teaspoon at a time, whisking continuously. (If the eggs are added all at once, they will literally "scramble.") Continue to cook the mixture over medium-high heat until it reaches a pudding-like consistency, about 5 to 8 more minutes. Remove the pan from the heat; whisk in the vanilla extract. Allow the custard to cool completely before filling the "well" of each cooled torte.

9. **For the whipped cream filling:** Chill both a metal bowl and wire whisk attachment for at least 30 minutes prior to using. In a large bowl, whip the cream with an electric mixer on high speed until soft peaks are just about to form, 1 to 2 minutes; add the vanilla extract and powdered sugar and continue beating on high until stiff peaks form, 4 to 5 minutes.

10. Fill the "well" of each cooled shell with the filling of your choice; garnish with fresh fruit, if desired. Refrigerate if not serving immediately.

Note: You can also use a springform pan lined with parchment paper; just keep the piped "walls" lower than the height of the pan or the cake may collapse.

Sunshine Angel Food Cake

The addition of egg yolks makes this cake a bit more robust than traditional angel food cake, so it holds up well to the addition of fruit or fruit syrup. Read the instructions thoroughly before starting this recipe, and don't bake it when you are in a hurry. It is a bit of a challenge, and the devil is in the details—but the results are worth it! The cake can be served plain, dusted with powdered sugar, or topped with a lemon cream cheese glaze. Save your orange peels and make candied peel for garnish! (See page 146.)

Ingredients

Yellow Batter:

1⅓ cups cake flour, sifted

½ teaspoon cream of tartar

1 teaspoon baking powder

Pinch of salt

5 large egg yolks (reserve 5 eggs, whites for white batter), room temperature

¾ cup granulated sugar

1 large orange, zest and juice (about ¼ cup)

1 teaspoon orange extract

1 large lemon, zest only (reserve juice for glaze)

2 tablespoons water, if needed

White Batter:

½ cup cake flour, sifted

½ teaspoon cream of tartar

Pinch of salt

5 large egg whites, room temperature

¾ cup granulated sugar

½ teaspoon vanilla extract

Lemon Cream Cheese Glaze:

3 ounces full-fat cream cheese, room temperature

1½ cups powdered sugar, sifted

1 teaspoon lemon zest

1 tablespoon fresh lemon juice

½ teaspoon vanilla extract

Lemon peel (optional garnish)

Fresh fruit (optional garnish)

Plan Ahead

1. You *must* use a *tube pan* for this recipe; a Bundt-type pan will not work. *Do not* grease the pan. Egg whites are the leavening (raising) agent in this recipe. The batter literally has to "grab" the sides of the pan to rise.

2. Separate the eggs and allow the egg whites to come to room temperature before beating. Don't overbeat your egg whites.

3. The cake will need to cool completely in the pan *upside down* on a wire cooling rack. If cooled upright, the weight of the cake will cause it to fall in on itself.

Directions

4. Preheat the oven to 325 degrees. A higher temperature won't cook the cake properly. Do not spray or grease the tube pan.

5. To make the yellow batter, sift together the cake flour, cream of tartar, baking powder, and salt. Set aside.

6. Using an electric mixer on medium speed, beat the 5 egg yolks until very thick, about 5 minutes; gradually add the sugar while continuing to beat. Increase the mixer to medium-high speed and beat for 1 to 2 more minutes, until the yolks are thick and pale and they look like a slowly dissolving ribbon when the beaters are raised.

7. Decrease the mixer to low speed; beat in the orange zest, ¼ cup orange juice, orange extract, and lemon zest. Add the sifted flour mixture. If the batter appears too thick to pour, add 1 to 2 tablespoons water. Set aside.

8. To make the white batter, sift together the cake flour, cream of tartar, and salt; set aside.

Angel food cake probably originated in the United States in the late 1800s. It is so popular that October 10 is National Angel Food Cake Day!

9. Use an electric mixer and a large grease-free bowl to beat the 5 egg whites on medium speed until frothy, 2 to 3 minutes. Add the sugar; beat on medium speed for 4 to 5 minutes, until the mixture forms soft peaks when the beaters are raised. *Do not overbeat.* Decrease the mixer to low speed; mix in the vanilla extract and sifted flour mixture until just incorporated.

10. Combine the two batters by hand, gently folding the white batter into the yellow batter using a large, wide spatula until no egg whites show.

11. Scrape the batter into the pan and spread it level. Bake for 45 to 50 minutes, until the top of the cake is golden brown and springs back when gently pressed. Set the pan *upside down* on a wire rack. Allow the cake to cool completely in the pan, then tap the bottom lightly; carefully run a knife between the cake and the edge of the pan to loosen, if needed.

12. For the lemon cream cheese glaze, beat the cream cheese with an electric mixer until fluffy, 2 to 3 minutes. Slowly add the powdered sugar, lemon zest, lemon juice, and vanilla extract; scrape the sides of the bowl, and adjust the amount of lemon juice to the desired consistency for icing. Drizzle the glaze over the cooled cake using a fork. Garnish with lemon peel and fruit, if desired.

Velvet Cake

This is a versatile, basic cake that's light and airy from beaten egg whites. Serve plain or dusted with powdered sugar, or enjoy with ice cream, chocolate sauce, or fruit and whipped cream.

Ingredients

1 cup cake flour, sifted

1 teaspoon baking powder

1 cup granulated sugar, divided (½ cup amounts)

3 large eggs, separated, room temperature

1 teaspoon vanilla extract

½ cup boiling water

Directions

1. Preheat the oven to 350 degrees. Liberally grease a 10-inch (10- to 12-cup) Bundt pan and dust with flour; tap the inverted pan to remove excess flour. Sift together the cake flour and baking powder; set aside.

2. Using an electric mixer with a paddle attachment, beat ½ cup sugar with the 3 egg yolks on medium speed until light in color, 2 to 3 minutes. Add the sifted flour mixture and vanilla extract, then the boiling water. Mix until all ingredients are incorporated.

3. In a separate bowl, use an electric mixer to beat the 3 egg whites on high speed until stiff peaks form, 4 to 5 minutes; slowly add the remaining ½ cup sugar. Gently fold the egg white mixture into the batter *by hand* so as not to knock the air out of the egg whites.

4. Pour the batter into the prepared pan and bake. Check for doneness after 30 minutes; it may require an additional 5 to 10 minutes, until a cake tester inserted in the middle comes out clean. Transfer to a wire cooling rack; cool in the pan for 10 to 15 minutes before inverting the cake onto the rack. Remove the pan and allow the cake to cool completely before adding any desired toppings or serve plain.

Blitz Torte

Moist cake, custard filling, meringue topping . . . what's not to like?
The Blitz Torte has been around at least since the 1920s and gained popularity
in the 1960s when it appeared in the Betty Crocker Cookbook.

Ingredients

Cake:

1 cup cake flour, sifted

1 teaspoon baking powder

½ cup (1 stick) unsalted butter, room temperature

½ cup granulated sugar

4 large egg yolks, well beaten, room temperature

1 teaspoon vanilla or almond extract

3 tablespoons whole milk or heavy cream, room temperature

Powdered sugar (optional garnish)

Fresh fruit (optional garnish)

Meringue:

6 large egg whites, room temperature

½ teaspoon cream of tartar

½ cup granulated sugar

Pinch of salt

1 teaspoon vanilla or almond extract

½ cup sliced almonds

Custard Filling:

2 cups whole milk, room temperature

2 large egg yolks, room temperature

½ cup granulated sugar

2 tablespoons unsalted butter, room temperature

Pinch of salt

1 to 2 tablespoons cornstarch

1 teaspoon vanilla or almond extract

Directions

1. Preheat the oven to 350 degrees. Grease the sides of two 8- or 9-inch layer pans and line the bottoms with parchment paper. Sift together the flour and baking powder; set aside.

2. Using an electric mixer on medium speed, cream the butter and sugar until light and fluffy, 2 to 3 minutes. Add the beaten egg yolks and extract (vanilla or almond). Alternate adding the sifted flour mixture with the milk. Stop the mixer and scrape down the sides of the bowl with a spatula to make sure all ingredients are well combined; set aside.

3. To make the meringue, use an electric mixer with a whisk attachment to beat the egg whites and cream of tartar on medium speed for 1 minute; increase to high speed until soft peaks form, about 4 more minutes. Add the sugar, salt, and extract (vanilla or almond); continue beating on high speed until glossy, stiff peaks form, about 2 more minutes.

4. Divide the cake batter between the two pans (the batter will barely cover the bottom of the pans). Spread or pipe each layer with half of the meringue; top with sliced almonds.

5. Bake for 25 to 35 minutes, until a cake tester inserted in the middle comes out clean and the meringue begins to turn golden brown. Transfer to a wire cooling rack; cool in the pans for 10 to 15 minutes. Carefully run a knife around the edge of each pan to loosen the meringue, if needed, before turning out the layers onto the rack to cool completely.

6. While the cake is baking, make the custard filling. To prepare the custard filling, heat the milk and butter in a saucepan over medium heat until simmering, stirring constantly. Remove the mixture from the heat before it comes to a boil. In a separate bowl, whisk together the egg yolks and sugar until the sugar dissolves. Return the saucepan to a low heat. Pour in the egg mixture a little at a

time to avoid curdling. Add in cornstarch a little at a time and whisk continuously until the custard thickens, 8 to 10 minutes. Whisk in the vanilla or almond extract just as you remove the saucepan from the heat. Allow the custard to cool completely before topping the cake layer.

7. To assemble the cake once the layers and custard have cooled, spread the custard filling on top of one cake layer; cover with the second cake layer. Dust with powdered sugar and garnish with fresh fruit, if desired.

Note for custard: Custard filling can be made up to one day ahead and refrigerated.

Note for meringue: Egg whites must be at room temperature for the best, fluffiest meringue.

Banana Cake

This is a scrumptious, lighter version of banana bread. Add some chocolate chips for your chocolate lovers. Enjoy on its own or drizzle with chocolate icing (there is no such thing as too much chocolate).

Ingredients

Cake:

2 cups cake flour, sifted

Pinch of salt

1 teaspoon baking soda

1 tablespoon water

½ cup (1 stick) unsalted butter, room temperature

1½ cups granulated sugar

3 tablespoons light or dark brown sugar, lightly packed

2 large eggs, well beaten, room temperature

1 teaspoon vanilla extract

2 ripe bananas, mashed

3 tablespoons whole milk or heavy cream, room temperature

1 cup chopped walnuts

1 cup chocolate chips (optional)

Chocolate Glaze:

1½ cups powdered sugar, sifted

¼ cup unsweetened cocoa powder, sifted

2 tablespoons whole milk or heavy cream, room temperature

1 teaspoon vanilla extract

Directions

1. Preheat the oven to 350 degrees. Liberally grease a 10-inch (10- to 12-cup) Bundt pan and dust with flour; tap the inverted pan to remove excess flour. Sift together the cake flour and salt; set aside. Dissolve the baking soda in 1 tablespoon water; set aside.

2. Using an electric mixer with a paddle attachment, cream the butter, granulated sugar, and brown sugar on medium speed until light and fluffy, 2 to 3 minutes. Add the beaten eggs and vanilla extract. Slowly add the sifted flour mixture a few tablespoons at a time. Add the mashed banana; scrape the milk and the baking soda mixture. Stop the mixer and scrape down the sides of the bowl with a spatula to make sure all ingredients are well incorporated. Mix in the walnuts and chocolate chips, and finish mixing by hand.

3. Pour the batter into the prepared pan; bake for 45 to 55 minutes, until a cake tester inserted in the middle comes out clean. Transfer to a wire cooling rack; cool in the pan for 10 to 15 minutes before inverting the cake onto the rack. Remove the pan and allow the cake to cool completely before adding a glaze or serve warm from the oven.

4. To make the chocolate glaze, sift together the powdered sugar and cocoa powder in a medium bowl. Slowly stir in the milk and vanilla extract a little at a time to make a smooth, pourable glaze. Drizzle over the cooled cake.

Applesauce Cake

This amazingly moist cake (made without any eggs) has just a hint of spice. Drizzle with a cinnamon cream cheese icing for a wonderful coffee cake. I made this one in a standard loaf pan, but a Bundt pan will work just as well.

Ingredients

Cake:

2 cups cake flour, sifted

1 teaspoon baking soda

1 teaspoon ground cinnamon

½ teaspoon ground nutmeg

¼ teaspoon ground cloves

1 cup (2 sticks) unsalted butter, room temperature

1 cup light or dark brown sugar, lightly packed

1 teaspoon vanilla extract

1 cup applesauce

½ cup raisins

1 cup finely chopped walnuts or pecans

Powdered sugar (optional garnish)

Cinnamon Cream Cheese Icing:

8 ounces full-fat cream cheese, room temperature

½ cup (1 stick) unsalted butter, room temperature

2 cups powdered sugar, sifted

¼ cup whole milk or heavy cream, room temperature

1 teaspoon vanilla extract

½ teaspoon ground cinnamon

Chopped walnuts or pecans (optional garnish)

Directions

1. Preheat the oven to 350 degrees. Liberally grease a loaf pan (6 to 8 cups) and dust with flour; tap the inverted pan to remove excess flour. Sift together the cake flour, baking soda, cinnamon, nutmeg, and cloves; set aside. **Tip:** Toss the raisins and nuts with just enough flour to cover them; this will help your add-ins stay evenly distributed throughout the cake.

2. Using an electric mixer with a paddle attachment, cream the butter and brown sugar on medium speed until light and fluffy, 2 to 3 minutes. Add the vanilla extract. Alternate adding the sifted flour mixture and the applesauce, then add the raisins and nuts. Stop the mixer and scrape down the sides of the bowl with a spatula to make sure all ingredients are well incorporated; finish mixing by hand.

3. Pour the batter into the prepared pan; bake 45 to 55 minutes, until a cake tester inserted in the middle comes out clean. Transfer to a wire cooling rack; cool in the pan for 10 to 15 minutes before inverting the cake onto the rack. Remove the pan and allow the cake to cool completely before dusting with powdered sugar or topping with a cinnamon cream cheese glaze, if desired.

4. To make the cinnamon cream cheese icing, use an electric mixer on medium speed to combine the cream cheese and butter until light and fluffy. Add the powdered sugar, milk, vanilla extract, and cinnamon and continue beating until smooth; add extra cinnamon, if desired. For a thinner consistency, add more milk; to thicken, add more powdered sugar. Drizzle the icing over the cooled cake; top with additional chopped walnuts or pecans.

Eggless Fruit Cake

This cake is not the heavy fruit cake most of us are used to. The original recipe only contained raisins; however, I have added chopped dates and walnuts at times to jazz it up. The dates give added moistness.

Ingredients

2 cups cake flour, sifted

1 teaspoon baking soda

1 teaspoon ground cinnamon

½ teaspoon ground cloves

½ cup (1 stick) unsalted butter, room temperature

1 cup granulated sugar

1 cup sour milk (see note) or buttermilk, room temperature

½ cup unsulfured molasses

1 cup raisins

1 cup chopped pitted dates (optional)

1 cup chopped walnuts (optional)

1 cup apricot jam or preserves

Directions

1. Preheat the oven to 350 degrees. Liberally grease a 10-inch (10- to 12-cup) Bundt pan and dust with flour; tap the inverted pan to remove excess flour. Sift together the cake flour, baking soda, cinnamon, and cloves; set aside. **Tip:** Toss any dried fruits and nuts with just enough flour to cover them; this will help your add-ins to be evenly distributed throughout the cake.

2. Using an electric mixer with a paddle attachment, cream the butter and sugar until light and fluffy, 2 to 3 minutes. Alternate adding the sifted flour mixture and the sour milk, then mix in the molasses, raisins, and optional dates and walnuts. Stop the mixer and scrape down the sides of the bowl with a spatula to make sure all ingredients are well incorporated. Finish mixing by hand that so you don't overmix.

3. Pour the batter into the prepared pan; bake for 45 to 55 minutes, until a cake tester inserted in the middle comes out clean. Transfer to a wire cooling rack; cool in the pan for 10 to 15 minutes before inverting the cake onto the rack. Remove the pan and allow the cake to cool completely.

4. To glaze the cake, warm the apricot jam in the microwave for 30 seconds; dab on with a pastry brush to thoroughly cover.

Note: To replicate sour milk, add 1 tablespoon white vinegar or lemon juice to 1 cup whole milk; allow it to stand for at least 5 minutes before using. Buttermilk can be substituted (omit the vinegar or lemon juice) and will give a slightly richer texture.

Devil's Food Cake

A classic favorite! The original recipe did not call for sour cream, but that addition gives it extra moistness. Enjoy this cake plain or try one (or more) of the add-ins for a delicious variation on a theme.

Ingredients

Cake:

2 cups cake flour, sifted

¼ cup unsweetened cocoa powder (light or dark), sifted

1 teaspoon baking soda

½ cup (1 stick) unsalted butter, room temperature

1 cup light brown sugar, lightly packed

1 large egg, well beaten, room temperature

1 cup sour milk (see note) or buttermilk, room temperature

3 tablespoons sour cream, room temperature

1 teaspoon vanilla extract

Optional Add-Ins:

1 cup chocolate chips

1 cup chopped nuts

1 cup miniature marshmallows

Chocolate Cream Cheese Icing:

3½ cups powdered sugar, sifted

⅔ cup unsweetened cocoa powder, sifted

Pinch of salt

12 ounces full-fat cream cheese, room temperature

¾ cup (1½ sticks) unsalted butter, room temperature

1 teaspoon vanilla extract

1 to 2 tablespoons whole milk or heavy cream, room temperature

Directions

1. Preheat the oven to 350 degrees. Prepare a 10-inch (10- to 12-cup) Bundt pan or two 8- or 9-inch layer pans. Liberally grease the Bundt pan and dust with flour; tap the inverted pan to remove excess flour. Or if using layer pans, grease the sides of the pans and line the bottoms with parchment paper. Sift together the cake flour, cocoa powder, and baking soda; set aside.

2. Using an electric mixer with a paddle attachment, cream the butter and brown sugar on medium speed until light and fluffy, 2 to 3 minutes; add the beaten egg. Alternate adding the sifted flour mixture and the sour milk. Add the sour cream and vanilla extract; mix until thoroughly combined. Stop the mixer and scrape down the sides of the bowl with a spatula to make sure all ingredients are well incorporated. Add any optional chocolate chips, nuts, or marshmallows, if desired; finish mixing by hand.

3. Pour the batter into the prepared pan(s); bake for 45 to 55 minutes for a Bundt pan or 25 to 35 minutes for layer pans, until a cake tester inserted in the middle comes out clean. Transfer to a wire cooling rack; cool in the pan(s) for 10 to 15 minutes. Then for a Bundt pan, invert the cake onto the rack; remove the pan. For layer cake pans, turn out the cakes onto the rack. Cool completely before icing.

4. To prepare the chocolate cream cheese icing, first sift together the powdered sugar, cocoa powder, and salt; set aside. Using an electric mixer on high speed, beat the cream cheese and butter until smooth and creamy, about 1 minute. Slowly add the sifted powdered sugar mixture, vanilla extract, and milk. Add more milk if needed to obtain the desired icing consistency. Spread the icing over the cooled cake.

Note: To replicate sour milk, add 1 tablespoon white vinegar or lemon juice to 1 cup whole milk; allow it to stand for at least 5 minutes before using. Buttermilk can be substituted (omit the vinegar or lemon juice) and will give a slightly richer texture.

The term "deviled" was coined in the eighteenth century to describe dark, rich, spicy, or chocolaty food.

Favorite Cake

I think I know why this is called "Favorite Cake." As basic a cake recipe as you can find, it is also extremely versatile. It makes a great backdrop for a decadent filling or flavorful icing—or both! Try adding in nuts, chocolate chips or sprinkles, or dried fruit, or even change up the extract. I filled mine with "from scratch" raspberry jam and topped it with seven-minute frosting and fresh berries. The possibilities are endless!

Ingredients

Cake:

2 cups cake flour, sifted

1 *tablespoon* baking powder

½ cup (1 stick) unsalted butter, room temperature

1 cup granulated sugar

2 large eggs, well beaten, room temperature

1 cup whole milk, room temperature

1 teaspoon vanilla extract

Jam Filling:

1 cup berries (blueberries, strawberries, raspberries, or a combination)

½ cup granulated sugar

1 teaspoon lemon juice

⅛ teaspoon lemon zest

1 tablespoon cornstarch

1 tablespoon water

Pinch of salt

Seven-Minute Frosting:

5 large egg whites, room temperature

2 cups granulated sugar

½ cup water, room temperature

1 tablespoon light corn syrup

½ teaspoon cream of tartar

1 teaspoon vanilla extract

Fruit or berries (optional garnish)

Directions

1. Preheat the oven to 350 degrees. Grease the sides of two 8- or 9-inch layer cake pans and line the bottoms with parchment paper. Sift together the flour and baking powder; set aside.

2. To make the cake, use an electric mixer on medium speed to cream the butter and sugar until light and fluffy, 2 to 3 minutes. Add the eggs. Alternate adding the sifted flour mixture with the milk. Add in the vanilla, then stop the mixer and scrape down the sides with a spatula to make sure all ingredients are well incorporated. Finish mixing by hand.

3. Divide the batter evenly between the two cake pans; bake 25 to 35 minutes, until a cake tester inserted in the middle comes out clean. Transfer to a wire cooling rack; cool in the pans for 10 to 15 minutes before turning out the layers onto the rack to cool completely before icing.

4. To make the jam filling, first rinse and drain the berries. In a saucepan, combine the berries, sugar, lemon juice, and lemon zest; simmer over a very low heat, 15 to 20 minutes.

5. Combine the cornstarch and water, then stir the mixture into the berries. Simmer until the sugar is completely dissolved and the berries start to soften; add the salt. Continue to simmer until the mixture reaches a jam consistency, 10 to 15 minutes; the mixture will continue to thicken as it cools.

6. Remove the berry filling from the heat; allow it cool to room temperature before spreading on the warm cake.

7. To prepare the frosting, heat some water in the bottom pan of a double boiler over high heat until the water boils (see note below); the water should not touch the bottom of the upper pan. While the water rapidly boils, whisk together the egg whites, sugar, ½ cup water, corn syrup, and cream of tartar

in the top pot of the double boiler until completely blended. Switch to using an electric hand mixer; beat at the highest speed for 7 minutes, until stiff peaks form. Do not overcook. Remove from the heat. Add the vanilla extract; continue beating for 2 minutes, until the frosting holds deep swirls.

8. Spread the frosting over the cooled cake. If desired, top with fruit or berries for garnish.

I lightly "torched" the icing with a kitchen torch to give it a toasted marshmallow flavor.

Note: Don't have a double boiler? Improvise! Cook the mixture in a heat-safe mixing bowl placed on top of a medium saucepan filled with water.

Rainbow Cake

This is similar to an angel food cake, but the butter gives it a moist crumb texture, and the addition of baking powder with egg whites helps it rise. I topped this cake with whipped topping and sprinkled some orange zest on top. The whipped cream will pick up the orange flavor from the zest.

Ingredients

Cake:

2 cups cake flour, sifted

1 teaspoon baking powder

Pinch of salt

1 cup (2 sticks) unsalted butter, room temperature

1 cup granulated sugar

1 teaspoon vanilla extract

¾ cup whole milk, room temperature

6 large egg whites, room temperature

1 teaspoon orange zest (optional garnish)

Whipped Cream:

1 cup heavy whipping cream, very cold

1 teaspoon vanilla extract

1 tablespoon powdered sugar, sifted

Directions

1. Preheat the oven to 350 degrees. Liberally grease a 10-inch (10- to 12-cup) Bundt pan and dust with flour; tap the inverted pan to remove excess flour. Sift together the cake flour, baking powder, and salt; set aside.

2. Using an electric mixer with a paddle attachment, cream the butter, sugar, and vanilla extract on medium speed until light and fluffy, 2 to 3 minutes. Alternate adding the sifted flour mixture and the milk until the batter is smooth.

3. In a separate bowl, use an electric mixer on high speed to beat the egg whites until stiff peaks form, 8 to 9 minutes. Gently fold the egg whites by hand into the batter mixture until evenly combined.

4. Pour the batter into the prepared pan; bake for 45 to 55 minutes, until a cake tester inserted in the middle of the cake comes out clean. Transfer to a wire cooling rack; cool in the pan for 10 to 15 minutes before inverting the cake onto the rack. Remove the pan and serve warm or allow the cake to cool completely before icing.

5. Chill a large metal bowl and the mixer's wire whisk attachment for at least 30 minutes prior to using. Whip the cream on high speed until soft peaks form, 1 to 2 minutes. Add the vanilla extract and powdered sugar and continue beating until stiff peaks form, 4 to 5 minutes.

6. Spread or pipe whipped cream onto cooled cake. Garnish with orange zest, if desired.

Apple Kuchen

Although "kuchen" comes in many forms, this version is more of a sweet dough than what we think of as "cake" in the United States. Topped with apples and cinnamon and drizzled with cinnamon cream cheese icing, this makes a great coffee cake or afternoon treat.

Ingredients

Kuchen:

2 cups cake flour, sifted

1 teaspoon baking powder

Pinch of salt

2 large eggs, well beaten, room temperature

1 cup granulated sugar

1 cup whole milk, room temperature

1 teaspoon vanilla extract

Apple Topping:

3 to 4 medium Granny Smith apples

½ cup (1 stick) salted butter, melted

1 teaspoon ground cinnamon

½ cup chopped pecans

Cinnamon Cream Cheese Icing:

8 ounces full-fat cream cheese, room temperature

2 cups powdered sugar, sifted

¼ cup whole milk or heavy cream, room temperature

1 teaspoon vanilla extract

½ teaspoon ground cinnamon

¼ cup additional chopped pecans (optional garnish)

Directions

1. Preheat the oven to 350 degrees. Grease the sides of a 9- or 10-inch springform pan and line the bottom with parchment paper. Sift together the cake flour, baking powder, and salt; set aside.

2. To prepare the apple topping, first peel, core, and coarsely chop the apples; combine the apples, melted butter, cinnamon, and ½ cup chopped pecans.

3. In a separate bowl, use an electric mixer on medium speed to combine the eggs and sugar. Alternate adding the sifted flour mixture with the milk and vanilla extract; mix until smooth. Stop the mixer and scrape down the sides of the bowl with a spatula to make sure all ingredients are well incorporated; finish mixing by hand.

4. Pour the batter into the prepared pan; spread the apple mixture on top. Bake for 30 to 40 minutes, until a cake tester inserted in the middle comes out clean. Transfer to a wire cooling rack; cool in the pan for 10 to 15 minutes before removing the collar of the springform pan. Serve warm or, if using the cinnamon cream cheese icing, allow the cake to cool completely before icing.

5. To make the cinnamon cream cheese icing, use an electric mixer on medium speed to combine the cream cheese, powdered sugar, milk, vanilla extract, and cinnamon until smooth; add extra cinnamon, if desired. For a thinner consistency, add more milk; to thicken, add more powdered sugar. Drizzle the icing over the cooled cake; garnish with optional chopped pecans.

Kuchen Fun Facts: *Kuchen* is the German word for cake. German cakes tend to be less sweet than traditional American cakes. The base of a kuchen is more like a pastry dough and often includes a fruit topping, such as apples, peaches, or pears.

Chocolate Cake

I almost called this the "Hung Jury" Chocolate Cake because my two sons-in-law, both professed chocolate aficionados, were equally adamant that the cake was either a bit too dry or just right. If you prefer a moister cake, add the optional sour cream. I paired this with a dark chocolate mascarpone frosting, which I feel calls for the cake to be less moist. You be the judge.

Ingredients

Cake:

2 cups cake flour, sifted

¼ cup unsweetened cocoa powder, sifted

1 teaspoon baking soda

½ cup (1 stick) unsalted butter, room temperature

1 cup granulated sugar

2 large eggs, well beaten, room temperature

1 teaspoon vanilla extract

3 tablespoons sour cream, room temperature (optional)

½ cup sour milk (see note) or buttermilk, room temperature

Dark Chocolate Mascarpone Frosting:

6 tablespoons powdered sugar, sifted

¾ cup unsweetened dark cocoa powder, sifted

Pinch of salt

½ cup (1 stick) unsalted butter, room temperature

8 ounces mascarpone, room temperature

1 teaspoon almond extract

6 tablespoons heavy whipping cream, room temperature

Sliced almonds (for garnish)

Directions

1. Preheat the oven to 350 degrees. Grease the sides of two 8- or 9-inch layer cake pans and line the bottoms with parchment paper. Sift together the flour, cocoa powder, and baking soda; set aside.

2. To make the cake, use an electric mixer with a paddle attachment to cream the butter and sugar on medium speed until light and fluffy, 2 to 3 minutes. Add the beaten eggs and vanilla extract; add the sour cream, if using. Alternate adding the sifted flour mixture and the sour milk until all ingredients are combined. Stop the mixer and scrape down the sides of the bowl to make sure all ingredients are well combined. Finish mixing by hand, being careful not to overbeat.

3. Divide the batter equally between the two cake pans; bake for 25 to 30 minutes, until a cake tester inserted in the middle comes out clean. Transfer to a wire cooling rack; cool in the pans for 10 to 15 minutes before turning out the layers onto the rack to cool completely.

4. To make the frosting, first sift together the powdered sugar, dark cocoa powder, and salt; set aside. With an electric mixer on medium speed, cream the butter and mascarpone until light and fluffy, about 3 minutes. Add the almond extract and mix well. Alternate adding the sifted powdered sugar mixture and the cream; continue to beat on medium speed until smooth. Add additional cream if a thinner consistency is desired. Top the cooled cake with chocolate mascarpone frosting; sprinkle with sliced almonds.

Note: To replicate sour milk, add 1 tablespoon white vinegar or lemon juice to 1 cup whole milk; allow it to stand for at least 5 minutes before using. Buttermilk can be substituted (omit the vinegar or lemon juice) and will give a slightly richer texture. The original recipe calls for sour milk. In the days of the Great Depression, nothing was wasted, so a cake was a good way to use up old or sour milk. In the spirit of the original recipes, I mainly use replicated sour milk.

Crumb Cake

A timeless recipe, this is a tender, moist cake with a cinnamon crumb topping. Serve plain at room temperature, or try it warmed with a scoop of vanilla ice cream.

Ingredients

1 cup (2 sticks) unsalted butter, room temperature

2½ cups cake flour, sifted

1½ cups light or dark brown sugar, lightly packed

1 teaspoon ground cinnamon

Pinch of salt

1 cup sour milk (see note) or buttermilk, room temperature

1 teaspoon baking soda

1 teaspoon vanilla extract

1 cup chopped pecans

Directions

1. Preheat the oven to 350 degrees. Grease the sides of a 9-inch square pan and line the bottom with parchment paper. Alternatively, use any shape pan or even a springform pan for this cake; avoid using a Bundt pan unless you want the crumb portion on the bottom.

2. Combine the butter, flour, brown sugar, cinnamon, and salt. Use your hands or a pastry blender to evenly distribute the ingredients as you would if making a pie crust until the mixture looks crumbly. Set aside 1 cup of the crumb mixture.

3. Add the sour milk, baking soda, and vanilla extract to the remaining crumb mixture to make the cake batter; pour the batter into the prepared cake pan.

4. Add the pecans to the reserved crumb mixture; stir until evenly combined. Spread the crumb mixture on top of the batter.

5. Bake for 25 to 35 minutes, until a cake tester inserted in the middle comes out clean. Transfer to a wire cooling rack; cool in the pan for 10 to 15 minutes before turning out the cake. Serve warm or at room temperature.

Note: To replicate sour milk, add 1 tablespoon white vinegar or lemon juice to 1 cup whole milk; allow it to stand for at least 5 minutes before using. Buttermilk can be substituted (omit the vinegar or lemon juice) and will give a slightly richer texture.

Midnight Cake

I'm not sure if this cake is named for its coloring from the dark cocoa or for one's craving a piece at midnight, but this is one of my favorite chocolate cake recipes. Rich and moist, it's flavorful enough to stand alone, or for extra decadence, top it with a chocolate cream glaze and sliced almonds.

Ingredients

Cake:

2 cups cake flour, sifted

1 teaspoon baking soda

1 teaspoon baking powder

½ teaspoon salt

1 cup (2 sticks) unsalted butter, room temperature

1½ cups granulated sugar

2 large eggs, well beaten, room temperature

1 cup hot water

½ cup unsweetened dark cocoa powder, sifted

1 teaspoon almond extract

Chocolate Cream Glaze:

2 cups powdered sugar, sifted

½ cup unsweetened cocoa powder (dark or light), sifted

½ cup (1 stick) unsalted butter, room temperature

4 ounces full-fat cream cheese, room temperature

⅛ to ¼ cup whole milk or heavy cream, room temperature

1 teaspoon vanilla extract

¼ cup sliced almonds (optional garnish)

Directions

1. Preheat the oven to 350 degrees. Liberally grease and flour a standard (8 cup) loaf pan or a 10-inch (10- to 12-cup) Bundt pan; tap the inverted pan to remove excess flour. Sift together the cake flour, baking soda, baking powder, and salt; set aside.

2. Using an electric mixer with a paddle attachment, cream the butter and sugar on medium speed until light and fluffy, 2 to 3 minutes; add the beaten eggs.

3. In a separate small bowl, slowly add the hot water to the cocoa powder; mix until smooth.

4. Alternate adding the sifted flour mixture and the hot cocoa to the butter mixture; blend in the almond extract. Stop the mixer and scrape down the sides of the bowl with a spatula to make sure all ingredients are well combined; finish mixing by hand.

5. Pour the batter into the prepared pan; bake for 45 to 55 minutes, until a cake tester inserted in the middle comes out clean. Transfer the pan to a wire cooling rack. For a loaf pan, cool completely in the pan, then turn out the loaf before serving. For a Bundt pan, cool in the pan for 10 to 15 minutes before inverting the cake onto the rack; remove the pan and allow the cake to cool completely.

6. To make the chocolate cream glaze, sift together the powdered sugar and cocoa powder; set aside. Using an electric mixer with a paddle attachment, cream the butter and cream cheese on medium speed until light and fluffy, 2 to 3 minutes. Alternate adding the milk and vanilla extract with the sifted mixture. Add more milk for a thinner, pourable glaze or less milk for a creamier, spreadable icing. Drizzle or spread the glaze over the cooled cake. Garnish with sliced almonds, if desired.

Brown Spice Cake

The original name of this cake was Brown Cake, but don't let the simple title fool you. This is a tender, moist cake with just a hint of brown sugar and spice. The trick is not to go overboard with the cloves. Top with cinnamon maple icing, or serve it warm—straight from the oven—with a glass of milk.

Ingredients

Cake:

2 cups cake flour, sifted

1 teaspoon baking soda

1 teaspoon ground cinnamon

½ teaspoon ground cloves

Pinch of salt

⅔ cup unsalted butter, room temperature

1½ cups light or dark brown sugar, lightly packed

1 large egg, well beaten, room temperature

1 teaspoon vanilla extract

1 cup sour milk (see note) or buttermilk, room temperature

1 cup raisins (optional)

Cinnamon Maple Icing:

8 ounces full-fat cream cheese, room temperature

2 cups powdered sugar, sifted

¼ cup maple syrup, room temperature

½ teaspoon ground cinnamon

Directions

1. Preheat the oven to 350 degrees. Liberally grease a 10-inch (10- to 12-cup) Bundt pan and dust with flour; tap the inverted pan to remove excess flour. Sift together the cake flour, baking soda, cinnamon, cloves, and salt; set aside. **Tip:** If using the optional raisins later, toss them with just enough flour to cover them; this will help the raisins stay evenly distributed throughout the cake.

2. Using an electric mixer with a paddle attachment, cream the butter and brown sugar on medium speed until light and fluffy, 2 to 3 minutes. Add the beaten egg and vanilla extract. Alternate adding the flour mixture and the sour milk until all ingredients are incorporated, taking care not to overmix the batter. Add the raisins, if desired. Stop the mixer and scrape down the sides of the bowl with a spatula to make sure all ingredients are well combined; finish mixing by hand.

3. Pour the batter into the prepared pan; bake for 40 to 45 minutes, until a cake tester inserted in the middle comes out clean. Transfer to a wire cooling rack; cool in the pan for 10 to 15 minutes before inverting the cake onto the rack. Remove the pan. Serve warm or, if desired, cool completely and top with a cinnamon maple icing.

4. To make the cinnamon maple icing, use an electric mixer on medium speed to combine the cream cheese, powdered sugar, maple syrup, and cinnamon until smooth; add extra cinnamon, if desired. For a thinner consistency, add more maple syrup; to thicken, add more powdered sugar. Drizzle the icing over the cooled cake.

Note: To replicate sour milk, add 1 tablespoon white vinegar or lemon juice to 1 cup whole milk; allow it to stand for at least 5 minutes before using. Buttermilk can be substituted (omit the vinegar or lemon juice) and will give a slightly richer texture.

Date Layer Cake

*This moist date cake with a custard filling and chocolate cream
cheese mirror glaze is sooo good. It's worth the calories!*

Ingredients

Cake:

2 cups cake flour, sifted

1 teaspoon baking powder

Pinch of salt

1 cup chopped pitted dates

1 teaspoon baking soda

1 cup boiling water

½ cup (1 stick) unsalted butter, room temperature

1 cup granulated sugar

1 large egg, well beaten, room temperature

1 teaspoon vanilla extract

½ cup whole or chopped walnuts (optional garnish)

Custard Filling:

¾ cup granulated sugar

Pinch of salt

2 cups whole milk, room temperature

1 teaspoon unsalted butter

2 large egg yolks, well beaten, room temperature

1 teaspoon vanilla extract

1 to 2 tablespoons cornstarch

Chocolate Cream Cheese Icing:

3½ cups powdered sugar, sifted

⅔ cup unsweetened cocoa powder, sifted

Pinch of salt

12 ounces full-fat cream cheese, room temperature

¾ cup (1½ sticks) unsalted butter, room temperature

1 teaspoon vanilla extract

1 to 2 tablespoons whole milk or heavy cream, room temperature

Directions

1. Preheat the oven to 350 degrees. Grease the sides of two 8- or 9-inch layer cake pans and line the bottoms with parchment paper. Sift together the cake flour, baking powder, and salt; set aside.

2. To make the cake, first combine the dates and baking soda; pour in the boiling water and mix well.

3. In a separate bowl, cream the butter and sugar with an electric mixer on medium speed until light and fluffy, 2 to 3 minutes. Add the beaten egg and vanilla extract; alternate adding the sifted flour mixture and the date mixture until thoroughly combined. Stop the mixer and scrape down the sides of the bowl with a spatula to make sure all ingredients are thoroughly combined. Finish mixing by hand to avoid overmixing.

4. Divide the batter evenly between the two cake pans; bake for 25 to 35 minutes, until a cake tester inserted in the middle comes out clean. Transfer to a wire cooling rack; cool in the pans for 10 to 15 minutes before turning out the layers onto the rack to cool completely.

5. While the cake is baking, make the custard filling.

6. To prepare the custard filling, heat the milk and butter in a saucepan over medium heat until simmering, stirring constantly. Remove the mixture from the heat before it comes to a boil. In a separate bowl, whisk together the yokes and sugar until the sugar dissolves. Return the saucepan to a low heat. Pour in the egg mixture a little at a time to avoid curdling. Add in the cornstarch a little at a time and whisk continuously until the custard thickens, 8 to 10 minutes. Whisk in the vanilla or almond extract just as you remove the saucepan from the heat.

7. To prepare the chocolate cream cheese icing, first sift together the powdered sugar, cocoa powder, and salt; set aside. Using an electric mixer on high speed, beat the cream cheese and butter until smooth and creamy, about 1 minute. Slowly add the sifted powdered sugar mixture, vanilla extract, and milk until thoroughly combined. Add more milk if needed to obtain the desired icing consistency.

8. To assemble the cake, arrange several paper towels under a wire cooling rack. Place one of the cake layers on the cooling rack; cover the layer with custard. Place the second cake layer on top.

9. Transfer the prepared icing to a large glass measuring cup or other microwave-safe container; microwave on high for 1 to 2 minutes, until it is a pourable consistency. Pour the warmed icing over the cake, starting in the middle; allow the icing to run over the sides. You may need to use a cake spatula to even out the glaze. Allow the finished cake to cool completely on the wire rack so that the icing will firm up.

10. Transfer the cake to a serving plate. Garnish with whole or chopped walnuts, if desired.

Sponge Cake

The biscuit sponge tends to be a bit drier than other versions of sponge cake, so for this recipe, I added a custard filling and topped the cake with whipped cream and fresh berries.

Ingredients

Cake:

4 large eggs, separated, room temperature

1 cup all-purpose flour, sifted

1 teaspoon baking powder

1¼ cup granulated sugar

½ cup cold water

1 teaspoon vanilla extract

Fresh berries (optional garnish)

Custard Filling:

¾ cup granulated sugar

1 to 2 tablespoons cornstarch, sifted

Pinch of salt

2 cups whole milk, room temperature

2 large egg yolks, well beaten, room temperature

1 teaspoon unsalted butter

1 teaspoon vanilla extract

Whipped Cream Topping:

1 cup heavy whipping cream, very cold

1 teaspoon vanilla extract

1 to 2 tablespoons powdered sugar, sifted

Directions

1. Preheat the oven to 350 degrees. Grease the sides of a 9- or 10-inch springform pan or two 8- or 9-inch layer cake pans and line the bottom(s) with parchment paper. Sift together the flour and baking powder.

2. Using an electric mixer with a whisk attachment, beat the 4 egg whites on high speed until stiff peaks form, 3 to 5 minutes; set aside.

3. In a separate bowl, use an electric mixer with a paddle attachment to beat the 4 egg yolks, sugar, and water on medium speed until thick and fluffy. Gently blend in the sifted flour mixture and vanilla extract. Stop the mixer and scrape down the sides of the bowl to make sure all ingredients are well incorporated.

4. With a spatula, gently fold in the beaten egg whites *by hand* until just mixed, taking care not to overmix (overmixing will "knock" the air out and prevent the cake from fully rising).

5. Pour the batter into the prepared springform pan, or divide the batter evenly between the two layer pans.

6. **For a springform pan:** Bake for 25 to 35 minutes, until a cake tester inserted in the middle comes out clean. Transfer to a wire cooling rack; cool in the pan for 10 to 15 minutes before removing the collar of the springform pan. Allow to cool completely. The cake can be used as is or sliced horizontally with a serrated knife to make two layers.

7. **For layer pans:** Bake for 15 to 20 minutes, until a cake tester inserted in the middle comes out clean. Transfer to a wire cooling rack; cool in the pan for 10 to 15 minutes before turning out onto the rack to cool completely.

8. While the cake is baking, make the custard filling. Combine the sugar, cornstarch, and salt; set aside.

9. In a small saucepan, heat the milk on medium-high until almost boiling. Whisk the sugar into the hot milk, stirring constantly. Cook until thickened, 4 to 5 minutes.

10. Gradually add the beaten egg yolks into the hot milk mixture, about 1 teaspoon at a time, whisking continuously. (If the eggs are added all at once, they will literally "scramble.") Continue to cook the mixture over medium-high heat until it reaches a pudding-like consistency, 4 to 5 minutes more. Remove the pan from the heat; whisk in the vanilla extract. Allow the custard to cool completely.

11. To make the whipped cream topping, chill both a metal bowl and wire whisk attachment for at least 30 minutes prior to using. In a large bowl, whip the cream with an electric mixer on high speed until soft peaks are just about to form, 1 to 2 minutes; add the vanilla extract and powdered sugar and continue beating on high until stiff peaks form, 4 to 5 minutes.

12. Spread the whipped cream over the cooled cake; garnish with fresh berries. Refrigerate if not serving immediately.

There are several types of sponge cake, with differences in the fat (butter) or leavening agent (baking powder) used. Traditionally, sponge cakes do not contain a leavening agent but depend on the incorporation of air into egg whites to make the cake rise; however, some sponge cakes are variations on this theme. The "biscuit sponge" was popular in early American cuisine, and this Sponge Cake recipe is similar to that, although this recipe does call for baking powder in addition to egg whites.

Jelly Roll

The jelly roll is always a favorite due to its endless versatility. Almost any filling can be used: fruit preserves (homemade or store-bought), custard, chocolate mousse—whatever you can think of. Take it up a notch with a complementary topping such as whipped cream, drizzled chocolate, nuts, or sprinkles. But whatever you choose, remember that the trick to that coveted tight swirl of the jelly roll is to roll up the cake while it is still warm, straight out of the oven.

Ingredients

Blueberry Filling:
1 cup fresh blueberries
¼ cup granulated sugar
1 teaspoon lemon juice
⅛ teaspoon lemon zest
1 tablespoon cornstarch
1 tablespoon water
Pinch of salt

Cake:
1 cup all-purpose flour, sifted
1 teaspoon baking powder
Pinch of salt
6 tablespoons melted butter
¾ cup granulated sugar
4 large eggs, well beaten
1 tablespoon cold water
Powdered sugar (for rolling the cake)

Lemon Cream Cheese Glaze:
3 ounces full-fat cream cheese, room temperature
1 teaspoon lemon zest
1 tablespoon lemon juice
½ teaspoon vanilla extract
1½ cups powdered sugar, sifted
Fresh blueberries (for garnish)

Plan Ahead

1. When making a jelly roll, the timing is critical once the cake is out of the oven. The cake needs to be rolled while it's still *warm* (so have a clean tea towel available to use); however the filling should be at *room temperature*. Be sure to make the filling ahead of time to allow time for it to cool.

2. To make the blueberry filling, first rinse and drain the blueberries. In a saucepan, combine the blueberries, sugar, lemon juice, and lemon zest; simmer over a very low heat, 15 to 20 minutes.

3. Combine the cornstarch and water into a smooth slurry, then stir the mixture into the blueberries. Simmer until the sugar is completely dissolved and the fruits start to soften, an additional 10 to 15 minutes. Add the salt. Continue to simmer until it thickens to a jam consistency (the mixture will thicken a bit more as it cools).

4. Remove the blueberry filling from the heat; allow it to cool to room temperature before spreading on the warm cake.

Directions

5. Preheat the oven to 350 degrees. Line a jelly roll pan with parchment paper. To make the cake, first sift together the flour, baking powder, and salt; set aside.

6. Cream the melted butter and sugar with an electric mixer on medium speed, 2 to 3 minutes. Add the beaten eggs and cold water, then the sifted flour mixture. Stop the mixer and scrape down the sides of the bowl with a spatula to make sure all ingredients are well incorporated; finish mixing by hand.

7. Pour the batter into the prepared jelly roll pan; bake for 10 to 15 minutes, until a cake tester inserted in the middle of the cake comes out clean.

8. Special assembly instructions: Lay a clean tea towel on a flat surface; sprinkle the towel generously with powdered sugar. Turn out the *warm* cake onto the tea towel; discard the parchment paper. About 1 inch from the end of the short side of the cake, cut an indentation halfway through the thickness (*do not* cut all the way through the cake). Starting at the short side with the indentation, roll up the cake in the tea towel as tightly as possible. Place the rolled cake seam-side down and allow to cool completely.

9. To complete the cake, carefully unroll the cooled cake and remove the tea towel (it will not be needed again). Evenly spread the filling across the entire cake, then roll up as tightly as possible, again starting at the short side with the indentation and finishing with the cake seam-side down.

10. To make the glaze, use an electric mixer on medium speed to beat the cream cheese until creamy; add the lemon zest, lemon juice, and vanilla extract until combined. Gradually add the powdered sugar, beating until smooth; thin with milk or cream to the desired consistency. Drizzle over the cooled jelly roll; garnish with fresh blueberries.

Variations: Use chocolate ganache, lemon curd, whipped cream, jam, or jelly for delicious filling alternatives. Or make the lemon cream cheese glaze into a frosting by adding an extra ½ cup powdered sugar; then pipe it onto the cake using a pastry bag with a star tip.

Marble Cake

Moist yellow cake with a spice swirl! This is an especially good choice for fall gatherings but is tasty any time of year. Drizzle the cake with cinnamon cream cheese icing for an added touch of sweetness.

Ingredients

Light Batter:

2 cups cake flour, sifted

2 teaspoons baking powder

¼ teaspoon salt

½ cup (1 stick) unsalted butter, room temperature

1 cup granulated sugar

2 large eggs, well beaten, room temperature

½ cup whole milk, room temperature

1 teaspoon vanilla extract

Dark Batter:

2 tablespoons unsulfured molasses

1 teaspoon ground cinnamon

½ teaspoon ground cloves

½ teaspoon ground nutmeg

Cinnamon Drizzle Icing:

8 ounces full-fat cream cheese, room temperature

2 cups powdered sugar, sifted

¼ cup whole milk or heavy cream, room temperature

½ teaspoon ground cinnamon

Chopped pecans (optional garnish)

Directions

1. Preheat the oven to 350 degrees. Liberally grease a 10-inch (10- to 12-cup) Bundt pan and dust with flour; tap the inverted pan to remove excess flour. Sift together the cake flour, baking powder, and salt; set aside.

2. Using an electric mixer with a paddle attachment, cream the butter and sugar on medium speed until light and fluffy, 2 to 3 minutes. Add the eggs; alternate adding the sifted flour mixture and the milk. Mix until smooth, then add the vanilla extract until evenly combined. Reserve ¾ cup of the light batter; pour the remainder of the light batter into the prepared pan.

3. To make the dark batter, combine the reserved ¾ cup of light batter with the molasses, cinnamon, cloves, and nutmeg until evenly mixed. Drop the dark batter by spoonfuls on top of the light batter. Use a knife to swirl the dark batter into the light batter for a marble effect throughout.

4. Bake for 45 to 55 minutes, until a cake tester inserted in the middle of the cake comes out clean. Transfer to a wire cooling rack; cool in the pan for 10 to 15 minutes before inverting the cake onto the rack. Remove the pan and allow the cake to cool completely before icing or dusting with powdered sugar.

5. To make the cinnamon cream cheese icing, use an electric mixer on medium speed to combine the cream cheese, powdered sugar, milk, and cinnamon until smooth; add extra cinnamon, if desired. For thinner consistency, add more milk; to thicken, add more powdered sugar. Drizzle the icing over the cooled cake; top with chopped pecans, if desired.

PIES

THOUGHTS ON PIES

I am really surprised at how few pie recipes there were in the original cookbook—five in all: pumpkin, poppy seed, caramel, banana, and lemon. This may support my theory that the original author lived in an urban area, as there is no cherry pie, no apple pie, no peach pie... nothing made with what I would think would be common in a rural home.

Pies would be an easy source of calories for the hardworking rural family. All the baker would need to do is put some fruit into a pie crust. Pie crust would have been straight lard (or perhaps half butter, half lard), water, and flour. Apples, pears, or peaches probably would have been easy to come by, either fresh in the summer or from fruits canned for the winter.

Notably, none of the original recipes had directions for a pie crust because back then it was assumed that every baker knew how to make a pie crust. However, I added my favorite Sweet Pie Crust recipe for you to enjoy and included both blind-bake and par-bake directions. Feel free to use a store-bought pie crust or substitute your own favorite recipe from scratch.

7:45 a.m. Tip Estes' children watch their mother make a pie. Near Fowler, Indiana

Lee, R., photographer. (1937) www.loc.gov/item/2017763749

PIE CRUST HINTS

There are already many well-written instructions on how to make a pie crust, so these are the hints that I feel are most important. See the reference list at the back for my go-to cookbook authors.

Here are four steps to making great pie crust:

1. **Make the dough.** Unless you already have a favorite pie crust recipe you want to try, you can't go wrong with using my Sweet Pie Crust recipe included in this section to make your dough.

2. **Chill the dough.** Once you have made the dough, flatten it into a disc, cover with plastic wrap, and refrigerate for at least 30 minutes and no more than 3 hours prior to rolling it out.

   The dough can actually be made ahead and chilled up to two days, tightly wrapped in plastic wrap in the refrigerator, or you can freeze it up to three months. After this point, it's best to start over.

   A chilled marble or stone surface will help your dough stay cooler as you roll it out. I have a marble cutting board that I freeze for 15 to 20 minutes before I use it, so be sure to plan ahead if you'd like to do that. (Be sure your chilled dough has been out of the refrigerator for at least 1 to 2 hours before rolling it out.)

3. **Roll out the dough.** There are many different types of rolling pins. After some experimentation, I discovered that I prefer a tapered French rolling pin, but you may have a different personal preference.

   Roll out your dough between ⅛- and ¼-inch thick on a surface that has been lightly dusted with flour (using too much flour can make your dough dry). When I began making my own pie crusts, I measured the thickness of the dough with a small plastic ruler that I kept with my pastry supplies, but eventually I learned to "eyeball" the thickness. The ruler also comes in handy for measuring the circumference of your pie dough, which should be at least 1 to 2 inches bigger than the circumference of your pie pan. If I need to be especially precise, I roll out my dough on a silicone baking mat with a circle imprinted on it.

4. **Blind-bake (or par-bake) the crust prior to filling.** It is a good idea to blind-bake your pie crust before filling to prevent the dreaded soggy bottom. A par-baked crust works the same way, but the crust is initially baked for a shorter time and will finish baking once the filling is added.

   To blind-bake the crust, transfer your rolled-out dough to the pie pan, smooth it down (crimp the edges if you are doing so), and use a fork to poke holes in the bottom crust to allow steam to escape while baking. Place a piece of parchment paper on top of the crust, and evenly fill with pie weights. Don't have pie weights? No problem. Uncooked (dry) beans or rice will work just fine. Be sure to spread the weights evenly across the entire bottom crust. Weighing the crust down while blind-baking or par-baking will keep the crust from bubbling up, blistering, puffing up, or shrinking.

Sweet Pie Crust

This is my go-to scratch recipe for pie crust. Omit the powdered sugar for a more savory crust if you like. Remember, there is nothing wrong with using a store-bought pie crust.

Ingredients

2 cups all-purpose flour, sifted

1 heaping tablespoon powdered sugar (optional)

Pinch of salt

½ cup (1 stick) chilled unsalted butter, cubed

2 large egg yolks

¼ cup cold water

Directions

1. Preheat the oven to 400 degrees.

2. Combine the all-purpose flour, powdered sugar, and salt in a bowl; add the butter cubes. Lightly rub the ingredients together with your fingers until the mixture is the texture of breadcrumbs. Add the egg yolks and mix with your hands. Slowly add the cold water; mix until you form a paste that leaves the sides of the bowl clean.

3. On a lightly floured surface, shape the pastry into a ball. Don't overwork or handle the dough too much or it can become tough. Flatten the pastry into a disc and cover with plastic wrap. Chill for at least 30 minutes but no more than 3 hours before using.

4. Roll out the chilled dough into a circle ½ to 1 inch wider than the pie pan (avoid using a glass pie pan, as the crust is more likely to shrink). Place your dough into the pan; use your fingers or a small pastry roller to smooth the crust up the sides of pan.

5. Fold under any excess edges of dough; crimp the edge of the crust with your fingers or a fork. Pierce the bottom of the crust several times with a fork to allow steam to escape and prevent the bottom from bubbling up during baking.

6. Line the dough with a large piece of parchment paper. Fill the pie pan to the top with pie weights or dried beans. This is critical to prevent the crust from shrinking in the oven.

7. **For a par-baked crust:** Bake for 15 to 20 minutes; remove the parchment paper and weights and bake an additional 5 to 10 minutes. The crust should be light brown and just starting to set but not fully baked.

8. **For a blind-baked crust:** Bake for 20 minutes; remove the parchment paper and weights and bake an additional 10 to 15 minutes. Make sure the bottom is set; it should be golden brown.

9. Cool the crust completely before adding the filling.

Herbert Hoover and woman with large pie outside White House, Washington, D.C.

Making and putting pie crusts into pie pans. Bakery, San Angelo, Texas

Woman with pie at White House, Washington, D.C.

Banana Pie

This banana pie is easy to make. The filling is rich and creamy, and the meringue makes an impressive statement. For the crust, make my Sweet Pie Crust recipe or prepare a store-bought pie crust. Serve this pie plain or top with fresh banana slices, whipped cream, or meringue.

Ingredients

Banana Pie:

1 blind-baked pie crust, cooled

1 to 2 large ripe bananas, sliced

6 large egg yolks, lightly beaten, room temperature

½ cup granulated sugar

¾ cup (1½ sticks) unsalted butter, room temperature

1½ cups whole milk, room temperature

2 tablespoons cornstarch

1 teaspoon vanilla extract

Meringue Topping:

6 large egg whites, room temperature

½ teaspoon cream of tartar

⅓ cup granulated sugar

Pinch of salt

1 teaspoon vanilla extract

Whipped Cream Topping:

1 cup heavy whipping cream, very cold

1 teaspoon vanilla extract

1 to 2 tablespoons powdered sugar, sifted

Plan Ahead

1. Blind-bake the Sweet Pie Crust or a store-bought pie crust according to the package instructions; allow to cool completely before adding the filling.

2. For best topping results, prepare the supplies in advance for the desired topping: Set out the eggs to warm to room temperature (if making meringue) or chill a metal bowl and wire whisk attachment for the mixer (if making whipped cream).

Directions

3. To prepare the banana filling, first line the prepared crust with overlapping layers of sliced bananas.

4. In a small saucepan over medium heat, combine the egg yolks, sugar, butter, and milk. Sift in the cornstarch using a cake sifter or sieve to reduce lumps. Cook until thickened to a pudding-like consistency, stirring constantly. Do not allow mixture to boil. Remove from the heat; stir in the vanilla extract.

5. Allow the filling to cool completely, then spread over the sliced bananas in the crust. Serve plain or with fresh banana slices, or top with meringue or whipped cream.

6. **For the meringue topping:** Preheat the oven to 325 degrees. Using an electric mixer with a whisk attachment, beat the egg whites and cream of tartar on medium speed for 1 minute; increase to high speed until soft peaks form, about 4 more minutes. Add the sugar, salt, and vanilla; continue beating on high speed until glossy, stiff peaks form, about 2 more minutes.

7. Spread the meringue on top of the banana filling, extending it to the edges to completely cover the filling. Cover the edges of the pie crust with aluminum foil, if needed, for this second baking. Bake for 15 to 20 minutes, until the meringue begins to turn golden brown. Cool completely before serving.

8. **For the whipped cream topping:** Chill both a metal bowl and wire whisk attachment for at least 30 minutes prior to using. In a large bowl, whip the cream with an electric mixer on high speed until soft peaks are just about to form, 1 to 2 minutes; add the vanilla extract and powdered sugar and continue beating on high until stiff peaks form, 4 to 5 minutes.

9. Spread the whipped cream over the cooled pie. Refrigerate if not serving immediately.

Note for whipped cream: Recipe may be doubled or tripled as desired. Other extract flavors may be substituted for the vanilla.

Note for meringue: Egg whites must be at room temperature for the best, fluffiest meringue.

Caramel Pie

Sweet and smooth caramel custard . . . in a pie! This is absolutely decadent! The original recipe called for a meringue topping, but I had better results either leaving it plain or topping it with whipped cream. For the crust, make my Sweet Pie Crust recipe or prepare a store-bought pie crust.

Ingredients

Caramel Pie:

1 blind-baked pie crust, cooled

1½ cups light or dark brown sugar, lightly packed

4 large egg yolks, room temperature (reserve whites for meringue)

2 cups whole milk, room temperature

1 teaspoon unsalted butter, room temperature

4 tablespoons all-purpose flour

1 teaspoon vanilla extract

Whipped Cream Topping:

1 cup heavy whipping cream, very cold

1 teaspoon vanilla extract

1 to 2 tablespoons powdered sugar, sifted

Plan ahead

1. Blind-bake the Sweet Pie Crust recipe or a store-bought pie crust according to package instructions; allow to cool completely before adding the filling.

2. If making the whipped cream, chill a metal bowl and wire whisk attachment for the mixer for the best results.

Directions

3. To prepare the caramel filling, use a small saucepan over medium heat to cook the brown sugar, egg yolks, milk, and butter, stirring constantly until it reaches a custard-like consistency, approximately 5-8 minutes. Do not allow mixture to boil. If the mixture needs to be thicker, sift in up to 4 tablespoons all-purpose flour using a cake sifter or sieve to reduce lumps. Remove from the heat; stir in the vanilla extract. The mixture will thicken as it cools.

4. Allow the filling to cool completely, then spoon into the baked pie crust. Serve plain or top with whipped cream.

5. For the whipped cream topping: Chill both a metal bowl and wire whisk attachment for at least 30 minutes prior to using. In a large bowl, whip the cream with an electric mixer on high speed until soft peaks are just about to form, 1 to 2 minutes; add the vanilla extract and powdered sugar and continue beating on high until stiff peaks form, 4 to 5 minutes.

6. Spread the whipped cream over the cooled pie. Refrigerate if not serving immediately.

Note for whipped cream: Recipe may be doubled or tripled as desired. Other extract flavors may be substituted for the vanilla.

Note for meringue: Egg whites must be at room temperature for the best, fluffiest meringue.

Pumpkin Pie

Imagine my surprise when I read the instructions for this pumpkin pie and realized there was no mention of pumpkin. Hmm . . . Most bakers during this time period probably used fresh pumpkin, although canned pumpkin was available as early as the late 1800s. Below are instructions on how to make your own pumpkin pie filling, or you can certainly substitute canned pumpkin puree. For the crust, make my Sweet Pie Crust recipe or prepare a store-bought pie crust. Serve this delicious pie plain, or top with whipped cream.

Ingredients

Pumpkin Pie:

1 par-baked pie crust, cooled

2 cups fresh mashed pumpkin or 1 (15-ounce) can pumpkin puree

1½ cups whole milk, room temperature

¾ cup light brown sugar, lightly packed

2 large eggs, lightly beaten, room temperature

1 teaspoon cornstarch

1 teaspoon pumpkin pie spice

1 teaspoon ground cinnamon

Pinch of salt

Pecans (optional garnish)

Whipped Cream Topping:

1 cup heavy whipping cream, very cold

1 teaspoon vanilla extract

1 to 2 tablespoons powdered sugar, sifted

Plan Ahead

1. Par-bake the Sweet Pie Crust recipe or a store-bought pie crust according to the package instructions; allow to cool completely before adding the filling.

2. To prepare a fresh pumpkin for pie: You will need 1 medium sugar pumpkin; these are small pumpkins found in most grocery stores once the fall produce is available. Cut the pumpkin in half lengthwise and discard the seeds. Place the cut side down in a microwave-safe dish; add 1 inch of water.

3. Cover and microwave on high until very tender, 15 to 18 minutes. Drain the pumpkin. When cool enough to handle, scoop out the pulp and mash enough to yield 2 cups of mashed pumpkin.

4. For best topping results, prepare the supplies in advance for the desired topping: Set out the eggs to warm to room temperature (if making meringue) or chill a metal bowl and wire whisk attachment for the mixer (if making whipped cream).

Note for whipped cream: Recipe may be doubled or tripled as desired. Other extract flavors may be substituted for the vanilla.

Directions

5. To prepare the pumpkin filling, first preheat the oven to 425 degrees.

6. In a medium bowl with a whisk or electric mixer, combine the pumpkin, milk, brown sugar, eggs, cornstarch, pumpkin pie spice, cinnamon, and pinch of salt until thoroughly blended.

7. Pour the mixture into the prepared pie crust. Bake at 425 degrees for approximately 15 minutes, then reduce the temperature to 350 degrees; bake until a knife inserted in the center comes out clean, 40 to 50 minutes longer. Cover the edges loosely with foil during the last 30 minutes if needed to prevent overbrowning. Cool the pie on a wire rack.

8. Serve the pie plain, garnish with pecans, or top with whipped cream.

9. **For the whipped cream topping:** Chill both a metal bowl and wire whisk attachment for at least 30 minutes prior to using. In a large bowl, whip the cream with an electric mixer on high speed until soft peaks are just about to form, 1 to 2 minutes; add the vanilla extract and powdered sugar and continue beating on high until stiff peaks form, 4 to 5 minutes.

10. Spread the whipped cream over the cooled pie. Refrigerate if not serving immediately.

Lemon Pie

The filling of this pie is very similar to lemon curd and is prepared in the same way. Break out your double boiler (see note) and get ready for a lot of whisking! For the crust, make my Sweet Pie Crust recipe or prepare a store-bought pie crust. Choose either meringue or whipped cream topping to complete this pie.

Ingredients

Lemon Pie:

1 par-baked pie crust, cooled

1½ cups water

2 large eggs, room temperature

1 cup granulated sugar

2 large lemons, zest and juice

2 tablespoons cornstarch, if needed

2 tablespoons unsalted butter, room temperature

Candied lemon peel (optional garnish) see page 146

Meringue Topping:

6 large egg whites, room temperature

½ teaspoon cream of tartar

⅓ cup granulated sugar

1 teaspoon vanilla extract

Pinch of salt

Whipped Cream Topping:

1 cup heavy whipping cream, very cold

1 teaspoon vanilla extract

1 to 2 tablespoons powdered sugar, sifted

Plan Ahead

1. Par-bake the Sweet Pie Crust recipe or a store-bought pie crust according to the package instructions; allow to cool completely before adding the filling.

2. For best topping results, prepare the supplies in advance for the desired topping: Set out the eggs to warm to room temperature (if making meringue) or chill a metal bowl and wire whisk attachment for the mixer (if making whipped cream). Save the left over lemon peels to make candied peel.

Directions

3. To prepare the lemon filling, first preheat the oven to 350 degrees.

4. Whisk together the water, eggs, sugar, lemon zest, and lemon juice in the top pot of a double boiler (see note below) until completely blended. Constant whisking prevents the egg yolks from curdling. As the curd cooks, continue whisking until thickened to a pudding consistency, about 10 minutes; if the mixture is not thickening, sift in the cornstarch using a cake sifter or sieve to reduce lumps. Remove from the heat.

5. Cut the butter into 6 pieces, then whisk the butter into the warm curd until the butter melts.

6. Pour the filling into the prepared pie crust. Bake for 15 to 20 minutes, a until set. Cool completely. Top with meringue or whipped cream and candied lemon peel, if desired.

Note: Don't have a double boiler? Improvise! Cook the mixture in a heat-safe mixing bowl placed on top of a medium saucepan filled with water.

Note for whipped cream: Recipe may be doubled or tripled as desired. Other extract flavors may be substituted for the vanilla.

Note for meringue: Egg whites must be at room temperature for the best, fluffiest meringue.

7. **For the meringue topping:** Preheat the oven to 325 degrees. Using an electric mixer with a whisk attachment, beat the egg whites and cream of tartar on medium speed for 1 minute; increase to high speed until soft peaks form, about 4 more minutes. Add the sugar, vanilla and salt; continue beating on high speed until glossy, stiff peaks form, about 2 more minutes.

8. Spread the meringue on top of the lemon filling, extending it to the edges to completely cover the filling. Cover the edges of the pie crust with aluminum foil, if needed, for this second baking. Bake for 15 to 20 minutes, until the meringue begins to turn golden brown. Cool completely before serving.

9. **For the whipped cream topping:** Chill both a metal bowl and wire whisk attachment for at least 30 minutes prior to using. In a large bowl, whip the cream with an electric mixer on high speed until soft peaks are just about to form, 1 to 2 minutes; add the vanilla extract and powdered sugar and continue beating on high until stiff peaks form, 4 to 5 minutes.

10. Spread the whipped cream over the cooled pie. Refrigerate if not serving immediately.

Poppy Seed Pie

Poppy seeds give this rich custard pie a bit of texture and just a hint of nut flavor. For the crust, make my Sweet Pie Crust recipe or prepare a store-bought pie crust.

Ingredients

Poppy Seed Pie:

1 par-baked pie crust, cooled

4 large egg yolks, lightly beaten, room temperature

2 cups whole milk, room temperature

1 cup granulated sugar

2 tablespoons poppy seeds

2 tablespoons all-purpose flour

1 teaspoon vanilla or lemon extract

Meringue Topping:

6 large egg whites, room temperature

½ teaspoon cream of tartar

⅓ cup granulated sugar

1 teaspoon vanilla extract

Pinch of salt

Plan Ahead

1. Par-bake the Sweet Pie Crust recipe or a store-bought pie crust according to the package instructions; allow to cool completely before adding the filling.

2. Set out the eggs to warm to room temperature for best meringue results.

Directions

3. To prepare the poppy seed filling, first preheat the oven to 350 degrees.

4. Combine the egg yolks, milk, sugar, poppy seeds, all-purpose flour, and vanilla extract until smooth. Pour into the prepared pie crust.

5. Bake at 350 degrees for 20 minutes. Remove the pie; decrease the oven temperature to 325 degrees.

6. While the filled pie is baking, make the meringue. Using an electric mixer with a whisk attachment, beat the egg whites and cream of tartar on medium speed for 1 minute; increase to high speed until soft peaks form, about 4 more minutes. Add the sugar salt and vanilla; continue beating on high speed until glossy, stiff peaks form, about 2 more minutes.

7. Spread the meringue on top of the poppy seed filling, extending it to the edges to completely cover the filling. Cover the edges of the pie crust with aluminum foil, if needed, for this second baking. Bake at 325 degrees for 15 to 20 minutes, until the meringue begins to turn golden brown. Cool completely before serving.

Note for meringue: Egg whites must be at room temperature for the best, fluffiest meringue.

COOKIES & CANDY

Date Bars

I thought I didn't like dates—then I tried these bars. This recipe is always a big hit! The dates are just the right not-too-gooey consistency to make this a moist treat that is not overly sweet. No butter needed; these bars melt in your mouth! If you are taking these to the office, you might want to make two batches.

Ingredients

1 cup cake flour, sifted

1 tablespoon baking powder

3 large eggs, well beaten, room temperature

1 cup granulated sugar

½ cup pitted dates, chopped

½ cup chopped walnuts

Powdered sugar (for dusting)

Directions

1. Preheat the oven to 350 degrees. Grease the sides of a 9 x 13-inch cake pan and line the bottom with parchment paper. Sift together the cake flour and baking powder.

2. Mix the eggs and sugar either by hand or with an electric mixer with a paddle attachment. Add the sifted flour mixture, then mix in the dates and walnuts until thoroughly combined.

3. Spread the mixture evenly in the prepared pan; bake for 20 minutes, until just lightly browned. Allow to cool slightly before cutting into bars. Dust the bars generously with powdered sugar.

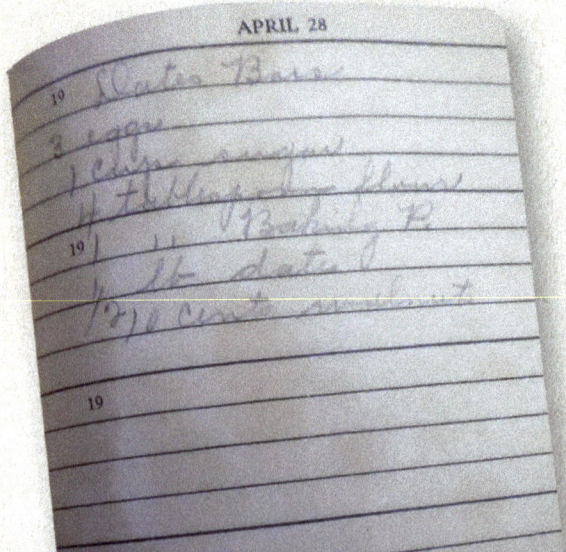

Anise Cookies

I was skeptical when I first made these because I am not a fan of licorice. However, the hint of licorice from the anise extract combined with the almonds and candied citron is absolutely delightful. Just a bit chewy, these "must try" cookies make for a beautiful presentation with the almonds and citron peeking out from the white cookie dough. Trust me on this one!

Ingredients

3 cups all-purpose flour, sifted

1 teaspoon baking powder

½ cup (1 stick) unsalted butter, room temperature

2 cups granulated sugar

4 large eggs, well beaten, room temperature

1 teaspoon anise extract

1 cup sliced almonds

½ cup diced candied citron (see note)

Directions

4. Preheat the oven to 350 degrees. Line a cookie sheet with parchment paper. Sift together the flour and baking powder; set aside.

5. Using an electric mixer with a paddle attachment, cream the butter and sugar on medium speed until smooth. Add the eggs and beat until light and fluffy, 2 to 3 minutes. Add the anise extract, then the sifted flour mixture; gently mix in the sliced almonds and the candied citron.

6. Chill the dough for at least 30 minutes in the refrigerator to decrease spreading when baking.

7. With a spoon or a cookie dough scoop, drop the dough by spoonfuls onto the prepared cookie sheet, leaving at least 1 inch between cookies to allow for spreading.

8. Bake for 8 to 10 minutes, until the edges just turn golden brown. Transfer the cookies to a wire rack; cool completely before serving.

Note: Candied citron can often be found in grocery stores around the holidays, but it can be ordered online year-round.

Butterscotch Cookies

These cookies are wonderful for peanut lovers! They are just soft enough, with the perfect balance of butterscotch flavor from the butter and brown sugar.

Ingredients

4 cups all-purpose flour, sifted

1 teaspoon cream of tartar

1 cup finely chopped roasted unsalted peanuts

1 teaspoon baking soda

2 tablespoons hot water

1 cup (2 sticks) unsalted butter, room temperature

2 cups light or dark brown sugar, lightly packed

2 large eggs, well beaten, room temperature

1 teaspoon vanilla extract

Peanut halves (optional garnish)

Directions

1. Preheat the oven to 350 degrees. Line a cookie sheet with parchment paper. Sift together the flour and cream of tartar, then add the chopped peanuts; set aside. Dissolve the baking soda in hot water; set aside.

2. Using an electric mixer with a paddle attachment, cream the butter and brown sugar on medium speed until smooth; add the eggs and beat until light and fluffy, 2 to 3 minutes. Add the flour mixture, then the baking soda mixture and vanilla extract; mix until combined.

3. Chill the dough for at least 30 minutes in the refrigerator to decrease spreading when baking.

4. Drop the dough by teaspoonfuls or roll into small balls and arrange on the prepared cookie sheet; space the cookies at least 1 inch apart to allow for spreading. If desired, gently press a peanut half into the top of each ball of cookie dough.

5. Bake for 5 minutes, then lightly press down on each cookie with a floured spatula. Bake for an additional 3 to 5 minutes, until just lightly browned. Transfer to a wire rack; cool completely before serving. (But they taste great when warm from the oven!)

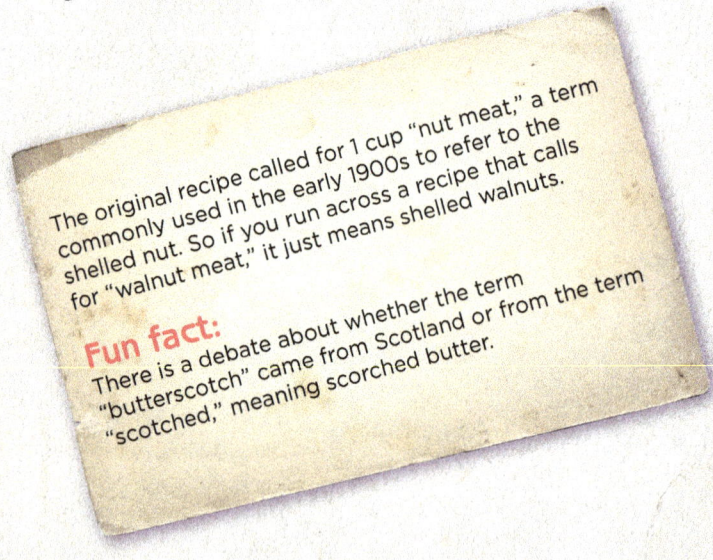

The original recipe called for 1 cup "nut meat," a term commonly used in the early 1900s to refer to the shelled nut. So if you run across a recipe that calls for "walnut meat," it just means shelled walnuts.

Fun fact:
There is a debate about whether the term "butterscotch" came from Scotland or from the term "scotched," meaning scorched butter.

Oatmeal Cookies

Everyone loves oatmeal cookies! These can be made with or without raisins. Walnuts can be added as well. I make mine with raisins, then place a walnut half on top for a bit of decoration.

Ingredients

- 1½ cups all-purpose flour, sifted
- 1 teaspoon baking soda
- 1 teaspoon ground cinnamon
- 3 cups old-fashioned rolled oats
- 1 cup (2 sticks) unsalted butter, room temperature
- 1½ cups granulated sugar
- 4 large eggs, well beaten, room temperature
- ¼ cup raisins (optional)
- Walnut halves (optional garnish)

Directions

1. Preheat the oven to 350 degrees. Line a cookie sheet with parchment paper. Sift together the flour, baking soda, and cinnamon. Stir in the oats until evenly combined; set aside.

2. Using an electric mixer with a paddle attachment, cream the butter and sugar on medium speed until smooth; add the eggs and beat until light and fluffy, 2 to 3 minutes. Gradually blend in the oats mixture until evenly combined, then mix in the raisins, if using.

3. Chill the dough for at least 30 minutes in the refrigerator to decrease spreading when baking.

4. With a spoon or cookie dough scoop, drop the dough by spoonfuls onto the prepared cookie sheet, leaving at least 1 inch between cookies to allow for spreading. If opting to add walnuts for garnish, gently press a walnut half into the top of each cookie dough drop.

5. Bake for 8 to 10 minutes, until lightly browned. Transfer the cookies to a wire rack; cool completely before serving.

Variation: For a slightly different texture, substitute granulated sugar for the brown sugar or use a combination of brown sugar and granulated sugar. Brown sugar has molasses in it, which tends to make the cookies softer and chewier.

Oatmeal Fun Facts:

National Oatmeal Day is October 29th
National Oatmeal Cookie Day is April 30th

Molasses Drop Cookies

This recipe reminds me of gingerbread cookies . . . only softer.

Ingredients

4 cups all-purpose flour, sifted

2 teaspoons baking soda

½ cup (1 stick) unsalted butter, room temperature

1 cup granulated sugar

1 large egg, well beaten, room temperature

2 teaspoons ground ginger

1 teaspoon ground cinnamon

1 teaspoon ground cloves

½ teaspoon salt

1 cup unsulfured molasses

1 cup boiling water

Directions

1. Preheat the oven to 350 degrees. Line a cookie sheet with parchment paper. Sift together the flour and baking soda; set aside.

2. Using an electric mixer with a paddle attachment, cream the butter and sugar on medium speed until smooth; add the egg and beat until light and fluffy, 2 to 3 minutes. Add the flour mixture, ginger, cinnamon, cloves, and salt.

3. In a separate bowl, combine the molasses and boiling water. Add to the dough and mix until evenly combined.

4. Chill the dough for at least 30 minutes to decrease spreading when baking.

5. With a spoon or cookie dough scoop, drop the dough by spoonfuls onto the prepared cookie sheet, leaving at least 1 inch between cookies to allow for spreading.

6. Bake for 10 minutes, then gently press down on each cookie with a floured spatula. Return the cookies to the oven and bake for an additional 3 to 5 minutes, until the edges are set and cookies are golden brown. Transfer the cookies to a wire rack; cool completely before serving.

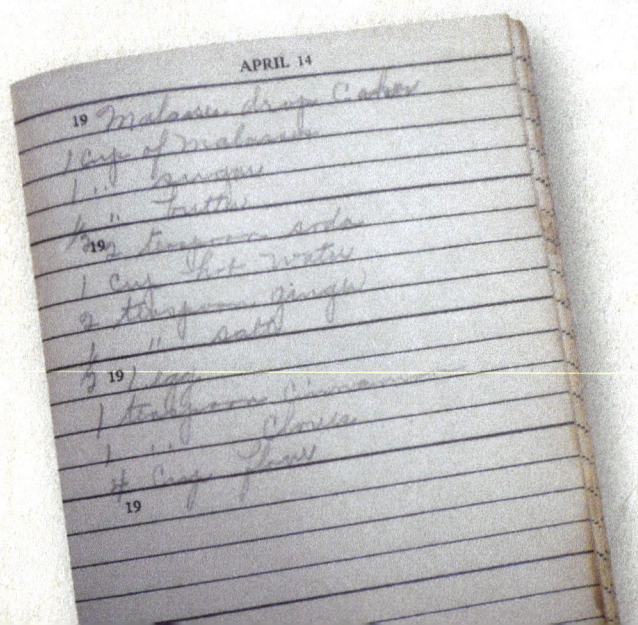

Chocolate Almond Cookies

The original recipe was called simply Almond Cookies even though it included the chocolate. These cookies are crunchy on the outside and soft on the inside—and taste great straight from the oven!

Ingredients

1 cup all-purpose flour, sifted

1 teaspoon baking powder

2 large eggs, lightly beaten, room temperature

1 cup granulated sugar

½ teaspoon salt

½ teaspoon ground cinnamon

2 ounces (56 g) milk chocolate baking bar, melted

1½ cups chopped almonds

1 teaspoon almond extract

1 cup sliced almonds (optional garnish)

Directions

1. Preheat the oven to 350 degrees. Line a cookie sheet with parchment paper. Sift together the flour and baking powder; set aside.

2. Using an electric mixer with a paddle attachment, beat the eggs and sugar on medium speed until smooth, about 2 to 3 minutes. Add the flour mixture, salt, and cinnamon. Add the melted chocolate, chopped almonds, and almond extract; mix until evenly combined.

3. Chill the dough for at least 30 minutes in the refrigerator to decrease spreading when baking.

4. Roll the dough into small balls; roll each ball in sliced almonds, if desired. Space the dough balls at least 1 inch apart on the prepared cookie sheet to allow for spreading.

5. Bake for 5 minutes, then lightly press down on each cookie with a floured spatula. Bake for an additional 3 to 5 minutes, until just lightly browned. Transfer the cookies to a wire rack; cool completely before serving.

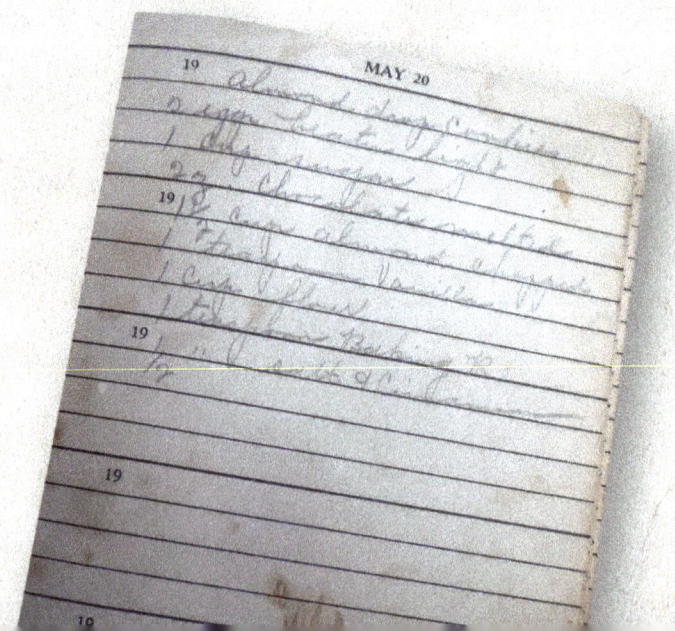

Cream Cookies

A creamier version of sugar cookies, these are delicious served plain or can be topped or mixed with almost anything. This is now my go-to recipe for Christmas cookies.

Ingredients

Cookies:

2¾ cups all-purpose flour, sifted

1 teaspoon baking soda

½ cup (1 stick) unsalted butter, room temperature

1½ cups granulated sugar

2 large eggs, well beaten, room temperature

½ cup sour cream, room temperature

1 teaspoon vanilla or almond extract

Optional Toppings:

Chopped nuts

Chocolate chips

Candy sprinkles

Directions

1. Preheat the oven to 350 degrees. Line a cookie sheet with parchment paper. Sift together the flour and baking soda; set aside.

2. Using an electric mixer with a paddle attachment, cream the butter and sugar on medium speed until smooth; add the eggs and beat until light and fluffy, 2 to 3 minutes. Add the sour cream and vanilla extract, then the sifted flour mixture; continue mixing until all ingredients are evenly combined.

3. Chill the dough for at least 30 minutes in the refrigerator (this makes the dough easier to cut and decreases spreading when baking).

4. Roll out the dough ¼- to ⬚-inch thick; cut the dough into shapes with your favorite cookie cutters, then transfer to the prepared cookie sheet, leaving at least 1 inch between cookies to allow for spreading. If desired, top the cookies with chopped nuts, chocolate chips, or candy sprinkles prior to baking.

5. Bake for 11 to 13 minutes, until the edges are set and just lightly browned. Transfer the cookies to a wire rack; cool completely before serving.

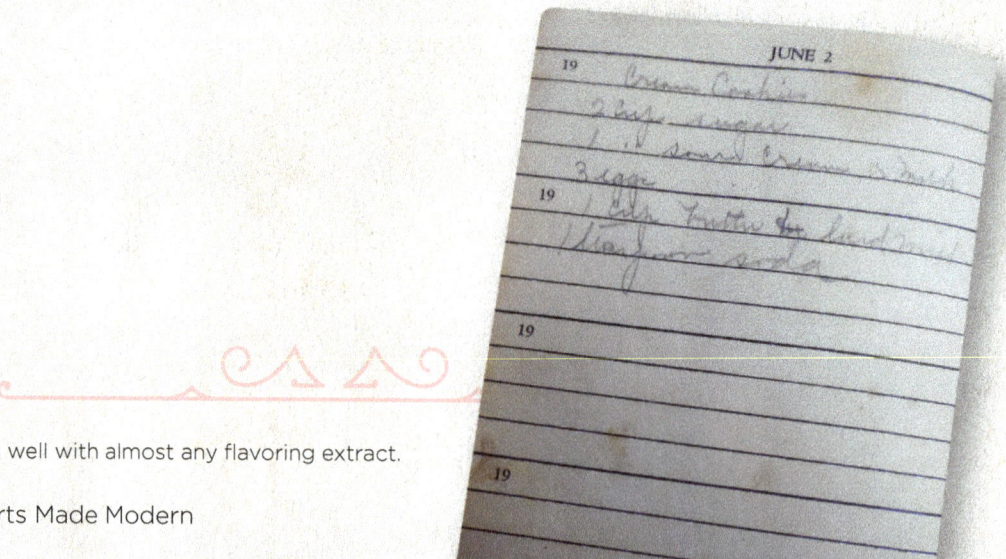

Variation: This recipe works well with almost any flavoring extract.

Finska Kakor

These Scandinavian cookies are rich with a texture like shortbread. While the original handwritten recipe was called "Finnoksa Kakor," I discovered in my research that this is a traditional recipe called "Finska Kakor," which means Finnish cakes.

Ingredients

Cookies:

¾ cup (1½ sticks) unsalted butter, room temperature

½ cup granulated sugar

1 teaspoon almond extract

¾ cup whole milk, room temperature

2 cups all-purpose flour, sifted

Toppings:

1 large egg white, slightly beaten, room temperature

1 tablespoon coarse sanding sugar

⅓ cup chopped almonds

Directions

1. Preheat the oven to 350 degrees. Line a cookie sheet with parchment paper.

2. Using an electric mixer with a paddle attachment, cream the butter and sugar on medium speed until light and fluffy, 2 to 3 minutes. Add the almond extract, then alternate mixing in the milk and flour until thoroughly combined.

3. Chill the dough in the refrigerator for at least 30 minutes (this makes the dough easier to cut and decreases spreading when baking).

4. Roll out the dough on a floured surface; cut strips approximately 2½ inches long and ¾ inches wide. (A pizza cutter works great for this.) Brush the top of the dough strips with the lightly beaten egg white. Mix the sanding sugar and chopped almonds; sprinkle over the dough strips.

5. Carefully transfer each strip to the prepared cookie sheet, spacing the strips at least 1 inch apart to allow for spreading.

6. Bake for 12 to 15 minutes, until the edges are set and just lightly browned. Be careful not to overbake. Transfer to a wire rack; cool completely before serving.

Honey Lemon Cookies

Honey and lemon are always a classic pairing. Not too sweet, not too tangy. These cookies are perfect with a cup of tea!

Ingredients

½ cup (1 stick) salted butter, room temperature

2½ cups granulated sugar

3 large eggs, well beaten, room temperature

¾ cup honey

4 cups all-purpose flour, sifted

1 small or medium lemon, zest and juice

1 small or medium orange, juiced

½ teaspoon lemon extract

½ cup sliced almonds (optional garnish)

Directions

1. Preheat the oven to 350 degrees. Line a cookie sheet with parchment paper.

2. Using an electric mixer with a paddle attachment, cream the butter and sugar on medium speed until smooth. Add the eggs and honey; beat until light and fluffy, 2 to 3 minutes. Alternate adding the flour with the lemon juice and orange juice; add the lemon zest and lemon extract. Remove the dough from the bowl and finish mixing by hand on a lightly floured surface, kneading in small amounts of flour as needed until the dough is smooth and doesn't stick to your hands.

3. Chill the dough for at least 30 minutes to decrease spreading when baking.

4. With a spoon or cookie dough scoop, drop the dough by spoonfuls onto the prepared cookie sheet, leaving at least 1 inch between cookies to allow for spreading. If desired, gently press sliced almonds into the top of each cookie dough drop.

5. Bake for 10 minutes, then lightly press down on each cookie with a floured spatula. Return the cookies to the oven and bake an additional 3 to 5 minutes, until the edges just turn golden brown. Transfer the cookies to a wire rack; cool completely before serving.

Cornflake Kisses

This is an easy and fun recipe! I add Christmas sprinkles in them for the holidays. Modern versions of this recipe often include flaked coconut.

Ingredients

4 large egg whites, room temperature

Pinch of salt or cream of tartar

2 cups granulated sugar

1 teaspoon vanilla extract

4 cups cornflakes cereal

1 cup flaked coconut (optional)

Candy sprinkles (optional)

Directions

1. Preheat the oven to 250 degrees. Line a cookie sheet with parchment paper.

2. Using an electric mixer with a wire whisk attachment, beat the egg whites on high speed until just frothy, 2 to 3 minutes; add the salt. Continue to beat the egg whites on high speed until firm peaks form. Slowly add the sugar and vanilla extract while continuing to beat the mixture. Stop the mixer.

3. Gently fold the cornflakes into the egg white mixture by hand, then fold in the optional coconut if using, taking care not to crush the cornflakes.

4. Using a dough scoop or a tablespoon, drop the mixture by spoonfuls onto the prepared cookie sheet. Top with a light coating of candy sprinkles, if desired.

5. Bake for 35 to 45 minutes, until the kisses are just turning light brown. Transfer to a wire rack; cool completely before serving.

Variation: Substitute 4 cups frosted cornflakes cereal (or even another sweetened cereal) for the plain cornflakes; decrease the sugar to only ¼ cup.

Seafoam Candy

Creamy nougat and pecans make this a delightful treat.
We call this recipe "Divinity" in the Deep South.

Ingredients

3 cups granulated sugar

½ cup hot water

¼ cup light corn syrup

¼ teaspoon salt

2 large egg whites, room temperature

1 teaspoon vanilla extract (see note)

⅓ cup chopped pecans

Plan ahead

1. You will need a candy thermometer and waxed paper or parchment paper. Check the weather: If it's a humid or wet day, the candy may turn out grainy rather than smooth.

Directions

2. Combine the sugar, hot water, corn syrup, and salt in a heavy 2-quart saucepan. Cover and cook until the mixture boils rapidly.

3. Remove the lid; put the candy thermometer in the pan. Cook without stirring until the mixture reaches 260 degrees; remove the pot from the heat and set aside. The mixture should be a thick, clear syrup. If cooked too long, the syrup will turn dark in color.

4. Using an electric mixer with a whisk attachment, beat the egg whites on high speed until stiff. Carefully pour the hot syrup in a thin stream over the egg whites, beating constantly with the mixer on high speed. Add the vanilla extract. Continue beating the mixture until soft peaks form and the candy starts to lose its gloss; stir in the pecans.

5. Drop the mixture by spoonfuls onto waxed paper. When the candy has set, store in an airtight container.

Note: For whiter candy, use clear vanilla extract rather than traditional vanilla extract.

Candied Citrus Peel

This was not one of the recipes in the original manuscript. In using all the fresh citrus fruit that many of the recipes required, I felt guilty for wasting all the peels! So in the spirit of "Use it up," I decided to turn these into candied citrus peel and found a recipe from daringgourmet.com. Candied peel makes a beautiful garnish for desserts, it tastes WONDERFUL by itself, or you can chop it up and use it as a mix-in for cakes and cookies. And bonus: You have also made some simple syrup, which can be used as a glaze for cakes or a flavoring for beverages or reused to make MORE candied peel!

Ingredients:

8 to 10 citrus fruits (can use oranges, lemons, limes or grapefruit. I would AVOID tangerines as their rind tends to be tougher and has less "pith".)

2 cups granulated sugar

1 cup water

Fine granulated sugar (for coating)

Directions:

1. Using a paring knife, peel the fruit, making sure to cut off the ends. The "white" part of the peel is called the "pith." It is bitter, but blanching will remove the bitterness. Make sure to include the pith in the peels as this makes the final product soft and chewy. Cut the peel into strips of the desired length and width.

2. In a large pot, boil the peels for approximately 15 minutes. This is called "blanching." Drain the peels in a colander and rinse well. Repeat this process 2 more times, using fresh water each time.

3. Using the same pot, combine the water and granulated sugar together and allow to boil until the sugar is dissolved. Add in the peel and reduce heat, simmering the mixture until the peels become translucent, approximately 45 to 60 minutes.

4. Remove a few peels at a time with a slotted spoon, allowing the excess syrup to drip off. Place in a separate bowl and toss with the fine sugar until thoroughly coated.

5. Your peel will need to dry thoroughly before using. This can be accomplished in several ways:

6. Set your oven to 120 degrees. Place a wire cooling rack on top of a cookie sheet, spread the peels on the rack, and dry in your oven for 4 to 6 hours.

7. Use a food dehydrator if you have one and follow the manufacturer's instructions for time and settings.

8. I have an air fryer that has a dehydrating setting, which set at 120 degrees will thoroughly dry my peels in about 6 hours.

9. You can also spread them out on a wire rack and allow them to air dry, but this will take one to two days.

10. Store the dried peel in an airtight container or Ziplock bag.

11. Be sure and save the homemade simple syrup you just made to flavor beverages or use as a food glaze!

Note: To make fine granulated sugar, put 2 to 3 cups of granulated sugar into your food processor with the blade set on the finest setting. Process for 2 to 3 minutes.

PARTING THOUGHTS

Every effort has been made to be as historically accurate as possible with this cookbook; however this is not intended to be a history book.

The historical significance of the original manuscript did not dawn on me until I realized that the date written on the inside cover was right in the middle of the Great Depression. I then began researching the era to get a better idea of who the original author was. The most regrettable part of my research is that I missed an opportunity: I lived with an actual survivor of that time period—my father, Pascal Simpson.

Daddy was born in 1918 and died in 1989 and would have been fourteen years old in 1932, the year the original manuscript was dated. I remember a few of his stories (he never forgave that cow for kicking over the milk bucket), but he never elaborated on what it was like growing up during this time. I wish I had known what questions to ask him and then taken the time to write down our conversations.

Almost everyone has a recipe that they cherish—one that reminds them of their childhood, a beloved family member (nobody could properly

My aim in restoring this manuscript:

1. First, to preserve this historically important document that miraculously wound up in my possession.

2. To revive an interest in what was arguably the most difficult period of time in modern history—if we don't learn from history, we will continue to repeat it.

3. To inspire others who still have family members who remember this era (they are few, and that number is dwindling rapidly) to record their stories before they are lost to us forever.

4. And last but certainly not least, to preserve those old recipes that are still in Grandma's recipe box or in the attic.

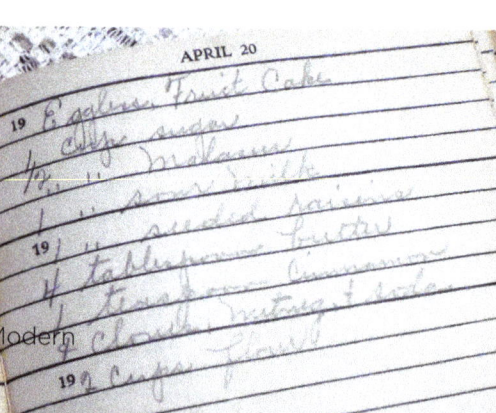

make my Aunt Jewell Ward's four-layer chocolate cake, even if she stood by you when you made it), or a special moment in time. I have literally hundreds of cookbooks, but the recipes I cherish most are the ones that came from Cousin Kelly or my best friend Tammy, written in their own handwriting on a recipe card or a scrap of paper. I have an album filled with these recipes. I may never cook or bake any of them, but I can pull out that recipe card and remember the time we shared it, and it's like a snapshot of that moment.

Since 2005, I have had the original manuscript that *Sentimental Sweets* was taken from. Over the years I worked on it from time to time. But when the pandemic shut down the world in March 2020, it gave me not only the gift of time in which to finish restoring the manuscript but also an appreciation for the family dinners we were no longer having. I spent the next three years restoring the recipes as well as researching the era.

The first time I walked into my local Walmart during the pandemic and saw the rows of empty shelves was the first time in my life I had ever worried about food, and at that moment I saw the economic parallels between the

> ## "The fondest memories are made when gathered around the table."

pandemic and the Great Depression: Many people were not working due to closed businesses. Many business owners could not weather these mandated closures and lost their businesses entirely. Fear and panic were common. Most tragically, loved ones were lost during this time.

I have gathered too much information and acquired too much memorabilia from the Great Depression to put into a 150-page cookbook. For further reading and information on the period, please visit my website at www.sentimentalsweetsbyval.com.

And if you run across an old recipe that you need help restoring, email me at valerie@ sentimentalsweetsbyval.com. I'd love to take a look at it and see if I can help you in its restoration.

BIBLIOGRAPHY

Galbraith, John Kenneth. *The Great Crash, 1929.* London: Penguin Classics, 2021. First published in 1955 by Houghton Mifflin (Boston).

Kasson, John F. *The Little Girl Who Fought the Great Depression: Shirley Temple and 1930s America.* New York: Norton, 2015.

Kyvig, David E. *Daily Life in the United States,*

1920–1940: How Americans Lived through the "Roaring Twenties" and the Great Depression. Westport, CT: Greenwood Press, 1997.

Nishi, Dennis. *Life during the Great Depression.* San Diego, CA: Lucent Books, 1998.

O'Shea, John Donald. *Memories of the Great Depression: A Time Forgotten.* Rapid City, SD: CrossLink Publishing, 2021.

Sandler, Martin W. *Picturing a Nation: The Great Depression's Finest Photographers Introduce America to Itself.* Somerville, MA: Candlewick Press, 2021.

Watkins, T. H. *The Hungry Years: A Narrative History of the Great Depression.* New York: Henry Holt, 1999.

Wormser, Richard. *Growing Up in the Great Depression.* New York: Atheneum, 1994.

Ziegelman, Jane, and Andrew Coe. *A Square Meal: A Culinary History of the Great Depression.* New York: Harper, 2016.

FOR FURTHER READING

To improve your baking skills:

Hoffman, Kristin. *Baker Bettie's Better Baking Book: Classic Baking Techniques for Gaining Baking Confidence*. Coral Gables, FL: Mango Media, 2021.

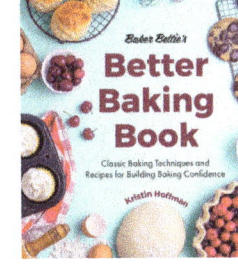

If you are learning to bake and only want to buy one book, this is the one to get. And don't miss Baker Bettie's "Mise en place" YouTube video—it will save your baking sanity!

To learn more about the history of cakes:

Byrn, Anne. *American Cake: From Colonial Gingerbread to Classic Layer, the Stories and Recipes behind More than 125 of Our Best-Loved Cakes*. New York: Rodale, 2021.

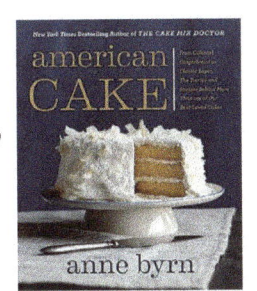

A stunning and in-depth look at the history of cake in the United States.

Ziegelman, Jane, and Andrew Coe. *A Square Meal: A Culinary History ofthe Great Depression*. New York: Harper, 2016.

Andrew Coe and Jane Ziegelman give an in-depth analysis of the political, social, and psychological impact of food, for nutrition as well as comfort, during a time when it was the utmost challenge to have enough of it. This book was instrumental in helping me understand what the preservation of the recipes in the original manuscript really meant.

To appreciate the challenges of period cooking:

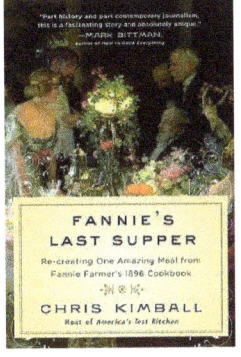

Kimball, Christopher, and Fannie Merritt Farmer. *Fannie's Last Supper: Re-creating One Amazing Meal from Fannie Farmer's 1896 Cookbook*. Toronto: McClelland & Stewart, 2010.

Fannie's Last Supper will give you a good idea of what it's like to try and recreate historical recipes, especially trying to cook on a woodburning stove.

To get lost in some period fiction:

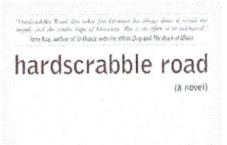

Weinstein, George. *Hardscrabble Road: A Novel*. Atlanta: SFK Press, 2018.

Hardscrabble Road is a wonderful novel set in rural southern Georgia in the Great Depression. The setting is not too far from where I grew up. (I wonder if some of my relatives may have inspired some of the characters in this book . . .) There is also a sequel, *Return to Hardscrabble Road*, that I plan on reading once this project is completed.

WAXED PAPER
in handy *"cutter"* box
no waste—easy to use

So simple a child can do it! Patented metal cutter on CUT-RITE box cuts the right length every time. Paper is waxed by special process, a double strength wax paper, yet it costs no more than the ordinary kind. Keeps food fresh, prevents odor spreading—saves work, time, money, food, health, hands. Ask your grocer for CUT-RITE, the *better* waxed paper. Continuous roll, 40 ft. long, only 10c.

with mayonnaise. Serves 8. *All measurements are level.*

JELL-O

REG. U. S. PAT. OFF.

SIX PURE FRUIT FLAVORS, LIME, LEMON, ORANGE, CHERRY, STRAWBERRY RASPBERRY

A Product of GENERAL FOODS CORPORATION

and so clean

PERFECT PIE CRUST
EASILY MADE

A good old-fashioned pie crust put in a package for convenient use. Contains the best quality flour, baking powder, shortening and salt.

Nothing to Add but Water

FLAKO takes the uncertainty out of pie crust making. Your pie crust always turns out right because the ingredients are ready mixed in the right proportions. A package makes a perfect 9-inch double crust. Delicious, convenient, dependable. If your grocer hasn't FLAKO

RED & WHITE

CAKE FLOUR

BAKING TRIUMPHS await you!
~ with scientific, controlled-speed electric mixing

Mixer-Beater Juice Extractor $19.50

IT'S LIKE
A SHEET OF PAPER...
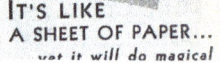
yet it will do magical

TRICKS in COOKERY

GOOD COOKING...

ROYAL
BAKING POWDER

SUN-MAID
PUFFED
SEEDED
MUSCAT RAISINS

SUN-MAID
NECTARS
SEEDLESS RAISINS

New

2 slice
Automatic Toaster $12.50
in Canada $15.75

With the new STAR-Rite you have only to set a lever and the toaster automati-

Ready now

ARM & HAMMER
CHURCH & CO'S
SODA
BICARBONATE
BAKING SODA

A 75¢ Value for 49¢
SEND COUPON TODAY

ENZO JEL

This useful aluminum ring mold sells regularly for 40c; holds 1½ pints; top diameter, 6¼ in.; depth, 2½ in.; strong, rust-proof; lustrous polish finish; molds most attractive salads or desserts.

Good Recipe Book Free

Now enjoy all the tempting salads and desserts that ENZO JEL provides—clear, sparkling, beautifully transparent—"Taste the Real Fruit Flavor." Our new book contains easy-to-follow, never before printed recipes for famous ENZO JEL combinations. Special offer is made to introduce ENZO JEL, tested and approved by the

a NEW lower priced model
KitchenAid
REG. U.S. PAT OFF.
Electrical Food Preparer for the Home

Slightly smaller than the older model

IN MEMORY

Pascal "Mr. Pete" Simpson
6/7/1918 – 1/18/1989
Born and buried in Dixie, GA

My father, Pascal Simpson, was born during WWI, lived through the Great Depression, and was a Sherman tank commander in the European theatre in WWII. (His tank was the last to cross one of the Rhine River bridges before it was blown up by the Germans.) He was a farmer, a college basketball player, a teacher, a soldier, and a rural mail carrier. He taught Sunday School at the Dixie Baptist Church where he also served as a deacon. Known as "Mr. Pete," he was loved by all; he was always cracking jokes and always saw the best in everyone. If he really liked you, you got a nickname (not confessing what mine was!). I will always miss him, and I regret not recording more of his stories or taking more pictures.

AUTHOR BIO

Valerie Simpson is a self-taught baker who turned her passion into a story worth sharing. Hailing from a peanut farm in Dixie, Georgia, where she first learned the art of baking perched on the kitchen counter watching her mother, Valerie has woven the rich tapestry of her life into every page. Her roots run deep, with a father who weathered the Great Depression on that same farm before serving in WWII. For over thirty-eight years, she's dedicated herself to the field of nursing, holding a master's degree in nursing, but her heart has always been in the warmth of the oven. Now residing in Palm City, FL, with her husband, Steve, three cats, and a spirited poodle, she finds balance between the precision of starting IVs and the creativity of baking. Her free time is a blend of adventures with her Paint mare Cali, transforming her yard into a sanctuary, and hunting for treasures in antique stores. Welcome to a slice of Valerie's life, where every recipe tells a story and every story is baked with love.

MARKETING PAGE

Visit SentimentalSweetsByVal.com to:

- Order books in bulk
- View additional recipes
- Receive baking tips
- Read Valerie's blog
- ...and more

www.ingramcontent.com/pod-product-compliance
Lightning Source LLC
Chambersburg PA
CBHW041536120626
46551CB00019B/2716